They Knew Too Much About Flying Saucers

GRAY BARKER

IllumiNet
PRESS

Library of Congress Cataloging in Publication Data

Barker, Gray.
    They knew too much about flying saucers / by Gray Barker
        p.   cm.
    Originally published: New York : University Books, 1956.
    Includes index.
    ISBN: 1-881532-10-0
    1.   Unidentified flying objects.
    2.   Human-alien encounters.

I. Title
TL789.B3   1996
001.942--dc21   96-46970

IllumiNet Press
P.O. Box 2808
Lilburn, Georgia 30226

10 9 8 7 6 5 4 3 2 1

Printed in the United States of America

They Knew Too Much About Flying Saucers

They knew too much about the wheel?

Introduction

He was six feet, four inches tall with a gentle southern accent and a sly sense of humor. His name was Gray Barker, and it can truly be said that he knew too much about flying saucers. After 1952, they dominated his life. On September 12th of that year a strange fireball came streaking out of the skies, crashing on a hilltop outside of the little cluster of houses known as Flatwoods in West Virginia. Seven young people climbed the hill and found themselves facing an eerie column of light that became known as "the Flatwoods Monster." Barker, a West Virginian entrepreneur, was among the first to interview the witnesses, and he chased UFOs, monsters and witnesses as a hobby for the rest of his life.

Within a short time after Flatwoods he established himself as the best writer in the UFO field. There was a poet's sensitivity about him which shone through the many books and articles he wrote. He became one of ufology's most articulate spokesmen. He corresponded with people all over the world, gathering some of the most puzzling reports of the next three decades and whittling them into stylish magazine pieces and books.

When I first met Gray, he was already a 15-year veteran of the Star Wars. Together we traipsed through the muddy fields of West Virginia in a series of bizarre adventures centered around the pursuit of a giant human-shaped entity with wings, known locally as "Mothman" or "The Bird" (We never caught it.) Later, he wrote a book about the episode with some added poetic touches titled *The Silver Bridge*.

He earned his living managing a movie theater and selling visual aids to schools. Gradually he created a sideline mail order business, publishing UFO books and hobbyzines, quickly becoming a familiar guest on radio and TV talk shows across the country. His first book, *They Knew Too Much About Flying Saucers,* was a sensation when it appeared in 1957. It towered over the mountain of poorly written cultist trash that had been cluttering the bookstores for half a decade. Gray carefully assembled the innumerable incidents involving mysterious men who had threatened UFO researchers, stolen films and other evidence, and stirred the latent paranoia in many of those who had taken an interest in the subject.

Was the government out to terrify teenagers and little old ladies into silence? Were the notorious Men In Black (MIBs) really government agents, or something much more sinister? Barker was the first to address this serious question.

Actually, aside from the frantic UFO wave of 1952, there wasn't too much happening in that decade. Very few people took a really active interest. There was Albert Bender in Connecticut (you'll be reading about his weird experiences in this book) and a housewife in Wisconsin named Coral Lorenzen. She founded a correspondence club called the Aerial Phenomena Research Organization (APRO) which managed to struggle through the 1950s with about 200 members. In June 1956, the leaders of the C.I.A. , Defense Department and general intelligence community in Washington, D. C. held a four day symposium on UFOs which was widely reported in the press. They felt something should be done on the civilian level so they founded the National Investigation Committees on Aerial Phenomena (NICAP). It quickly ran out of money—and members—and was eventually taken over by Donald Keyhoe, a minor bureaucrat with the Department of Commerce who had authored some flying saucer books.

Two men, Tiffany Thayer, a novelist and screenwriter, and Ray Palmer, editor of *Amazing Stories* and *Fate* magazines, really led the flying saucer hobbyist field until the mid-1960s. (It was, and is, basically a hobby confined to a relatively small group of people.)

Thayer, head of the New York Fortean Society, had started printing UFO reports in 1937. Palmer joined the fray in 1944, claiming in his editorials that all the governments of the world were engaged in a vast conspiracy to keep the public in the dark about arriving space ships. Keyhoe's early books in the 1950s were based largely on U.S. Air Force publicity handouts while Barker, Lorenzen, Palmer and Thayer were collecting new material and trying to make some sense out of what seemed to be a nonsensical subject. (Thayer gave up in dismay shortly before his death in 1956.) Barker clearly emerged as the best writer and for years contributed his "Chasing Flying Saucers" feature to Palmer's *Flying Saucers From Other Worlds* magazine (which began in 1957).

Meanwhile, the MIBs were popping up everywhere. After Barker's book was published he was inundated with letters from people who claimed they had also been harassed by the mysterious gentlemen in black suits and, often, turtleneck sweaters.

Since then thousands of MIB reports have been recorded in UFO publications all over the world. They continue to appear. Some are hoaxes but others are genuinely disturbing, almost demonological in content.

Gray passed away in December, 1984 after a long illness. He acquired a new-fangled computer and spent his last days working hard compiling an index to *Fate* and publishing some interesting collections of his works. But he has not been forgotten. A film tribute, *Whispers From Space*, was released in 1995. His massive files are on permanent display in a special room in the library at Clarksburg, West Virginia. And out there in the night skies those strange blobs of light still dance, perplexing new generations while men in outdated black suits sneak around isolated farms and deserted back roads.

Gray Barker's *They Knew Too Much About Flying Saucers* was just the beginning.

John A. Keel
New York City, 1996

Contents

A Hilltop, West Virginia   11
Flatwoods, West Virginia   23
Brush Creek, California   37
Lemuria   59
Points North, South and West   68
Jersey City, New Jersey   94
Bridgeport, Connecticut   109
Return to Bridgeport   125
Maury Island   136
Australia   151
Antarctica   160
California   177
Outside U.S.A.   197
New Zealand   210
Clarksburg, West Virginia   222
New York, Australia, New Zealand   236

Epilogue   245
Appendix 1: The Shaver Mystery   247
Appendix 2: Books About Flying Saucers   249
Index   253

1

A Hilltop, West Virginia

There are no such things as flying saucers.

The government has told you that. President Eisenhower himself stated to a saucer-conscious public that to his knowledge no one was coming here from another planet to pay us a visit.

If you believe in Donald H. Menzel, President Eisenhower, and Government announcements you need have no fear of being frightened by this story. Read it on a stormy night, or in the middle of a graveyard if you wish. Your equanimity will not be challenged.

Unless you don't believe in Donald H. Menzel, President Eisenhower, and government announcements.

In that case you just might be scared.

The "Flying Saucer Mystery," as it is termed, unofficially, by its investigators, is both entertaining and sobering at the same time. Humorous when its lunatic fringe is encountered, frightening when its apparent terrible realities are considered.

I used to laugh all the time about flying saucers. I thought they were the bunk. I still think that most of them are the bunk. But not all of them.

To me flying saucers were a lot of nonsense even when I heard about Captain Thomas Mantel, whose jet plane was shattered into smithereens by the planet Venus. I accepted the Project Saucer's report as the gospel about a brave man who was saucerdom's first martyr. I also believed that hallucinations often left burned patches on the ground after they had taken off.

I'm glad I wasn't around when one of these hallucinations came down practically in my back yard. It is better to be a live coward than a dead hero, and I have chosen the former alternative as a way of life. This particular hallucination scared seven of my neighbors almost to death. They had to clean one of them like a baby.

You laughed about the famous "West Virginia Monster" when you read about it in the newspapers. I'm glad you didn't see it, or you wouldn't be reading this. You wouldn't want to hear the word "flying saucer" mentioned again.

Put yourself into the shoes of a housewife, a teenager, or a 10-year-old boy and walk over a hilltop into the unknown. Into an experience so alien and awesome your body freezes, cold shock overcomes you and you later vomit for hours.

It is a calm, warm late summer evening when everything

seems normal and the way it should be. You are playing ball with some other kids when you see the meteorite, or at least that is what people said you saw.

It flashes across the sky and seems to land on the hilltop, as many meteorites seem to do.

"It didn't land on the hill. I'll bet it went on over," the neighbor kid says.

But you are kids and you decide to go up and look for it anyway. It is something to do, and the game is becoming dull. In that urgency peculiar to the undertakings of childhood everybody starts running.

"Maybe it's a flying saucer!" one kid shouts. Everybody laughs.

"Maybe it's a man from Mars and he'll jump out and get you!"

Everybody laughs again, for that is something you read about only in books—like this.

As you approach the hilltop you have a feeling you later are unable to explain to the reporters who talk with you. You smell a funny odor. You are afraid, but the others are along. And then you take comfort in the dog, romping along beside you.

Suddenly the dog tucks its tail between its legs and flees, yelping pitifully.

When you look over the top of the hill several things happen all at once. You see a fiery something totally outside your experience, and as you puzzle for a moment, focusing your eyes on the unknown, you fail to see the horror approaching from your left.

It is in shadow, but someone sees its eyes and flashes the light on it. It lights up like a neon sign!

To you this is not some phenomenon to be pondered and

examined rationally. You once saw Hell in a fever dream, or envisaged it in the choked rantings of a bleak-eyed evangelist. Here in a dread second is that same awful fear, though now all-consuming and elemental, grabbing your bones and muscles with cold convulsions.

It is a monster that walks like a man, a creature from the blackest memory of your fears. You don't remember when you started to run; not until later do you discover you are almost overcome by what someone said was gas.

Maybe this does read like a horror story, but in this respect the West Virginia "Monster" is at its best. And only if you can momentarily place yourself in the shoes of seven country folk who looked upon the unknown, can you begin to sift the imagined from the real; can you correlate the accounts and reach conclusions which may have truth in them.

If you were 10 to 17 years old, or if you were a housewife in a community where the supernatural has not yet taken on scientific explanations, just how would you describe what you saw?

How long did you really look at it?

This is a question I would like to answer, but that now is impossible. Does momentary horror strike an involuntary urge for flight, or are you frozen in your tracks for seconds, until your body can react?

At the most, the "monster" was observed from one to five seconds.

How much can you see in that length of time?

✱　✱　✱　✱　✱

I am neither a scientist nor a scholar. Nor am I a bookie, as some people misinterpret my occupation when I tell them I am a *booker*. I also tell them I operate the largest theatrical film buying-booking agency in the state of West Virginia. Charitably, no one else has started a film buying-booking agency in the state of West Virginia. I could even have made some money had it not been for Frankenstein. A Frankenstein's monster of my own creation—*flying saucer research.*

Now the monster has grown beyond all expected proportions. My desk overflows with clippings on saucer sightings instead of movie reviews; my filing cases on saucers are more extensive than the files on theatres. All of my spare time has been taken over, and I can only begin to cope with the mass of data and the correspondence, the pieces of the jigsaw puzzle containing the answer to the entire mystery—if it could only be put together!

*   *   *   *   *

The irate waitress should have jerked the paper from under the ash tray that morning of September 15, 1952 and hidden it. She might have saved me a lot of trouble—and work!

Waitresses are usually irate when they must set the orange juice down on top of an opened newspaper. But I was lost in thought, amazement, and disbelief. I was reading a U.P. story written in my home town.

POLICE SAY BRAXTON MONSTER
PRODUCT OF "MASS HYSTERIA"

SUTTON, Sept. 14—(U.P.)—Seven Braxton County residents vowed today that a Frankenstein monster with B.O. drove them from a hill-top near here, but police figured the smelly boogie-man was the product of "mass hysteria."

The thing, described by witnesses as "half-man, half-dragon," had not been reported seen since Friday night but residents of the area said a foul odor still clung to the hill-top yesterday.

All of this started when Mrs. Kathleen May of Flatwoods said she and six boys, one a 17-year-old national guardsman, climbed the hill to investigate her two small sons' report that a "flying saucer" landed there.

She said they found a "fire-breathing monster, 10 feet tall with a bright green body and a blood-red face," that waddled toward them with "a bouncing, floating" motion and sent them scurrying down the hillside.

. . . She said the monster exuded an overpowering odor, "like metal," that so sickened them they vomited for hours afterward.

"It looked worse than Frankenstein," said Mrs. May. "It couldn't have been human."

No wonder, in a listing of the ten biggest feature stories of the year, as judged by ABC, this phenomenon was described later as "the land-locked Loch Ness Monster." No wonder West Virginians, often credited with going barefoot, were heartily laughed at once again around the nation.

I didn't believe the story myself.

But then, I reasoned, a story as good as this one surely had some basis in fact. Such a story should be exposed, if it were a hoax. Better still I might get some publicity out of it.

Being a frustrated writer, I thought here was an opportunity to get my name in print again. Then, if I were doing an article for a magazine, I would have a logical excuse for going around questioning people.

Since *Fate* magazine, with which I was familiar, printed a great many articles about supernatural happenings, I decided to telegraph them, asking them if they were interested in a story. They wasted no time flashing back a wire:

STORY PROBABLY HOAX BUT INVESTIGATE RIGOR-OUSLY. DON'T SPECULATE SIMPLY STATE FACTS. 3 OR 4 PICS UP TO 3000 WORDS MONDAY DEADLINE.

I quote this wire to show the careful attitude *Fate* maintains about material it publishes. It was in the spirit of these instructions that I undertook to find out just exactly what had happened on that dark Braxton County hilltop.

You don't just pick up your brief case and leave a booking office at a moment's notice. Because of business problems I was unable to leave my office in Clarksburg, West Virginia, until Friday evening, exactly one week after the event had occurred.

Flatwoods is a small town with a population of only 300, six miles from Sutton, the county seat. I arrived late, but found an acquaintance's house lighted. I went in and he made some coffee.

This acquaintance did not believe the story at all. Some of the witnesses, as he put it, were "highly excitable." The skid marks editor A. Lee Stewart had seen were made by a tractor operated by Brooks Fisher, of Sutton, and the same tractor also could have left the odd, gummy deposits described as lying on the ground and foliage like oil.

At least I was getting my feet back on the ground. I had one lead, that of the tractor, to check.

Here was a story that could be checked separately with seven witnesses: Mrs. Kathleen May, a beautician; her two children, Eddie, 13, and Fred, 12; Gene Lemon, 17; Neil Nunley, 14; Ronnie Shaver, 10; Tommy Hyer, 10.

17

I went to bed determined to crack the story wide open the next day.

The next morning it developed that three people I wanted to see were not immediately available for interviewing. A TV show, "We the People," had contacted Mrs. May, and she, Lemon and editor Stewart were still in New York, after appearing on the program the previous night. They would return Sunday, I learned.

J. Holt Byrne, mayor of Sutton, and also editor of *The Braxton Central*, had first assured reporters and his constituency the phenomenon was caused by a meteorite, gases from which had almost suffocated the witnesses and might have formed an image they described as a monster.

But when I saw him about 10 A.M. he wasn't so sure, was ready to talk with Ivan Sanderson, a New York naturalist who had arrived to investigate the incident for a newspaper syndicate. Byrne suggested I first interview the Nunley boy and his grandfather, A. M. Jordan, of Flatwoods, with whom he lived. He had heard these people told a level-headed story. Later he was going to Flatwoods with Sanderson and look into the matter further himself.

The strange event had taken place simultaneously with sightings of aerial objects over several states. These, reported generally as meteorites, flashed across West Virginia, Ohio, Pennsylvania, Virginia, Maryland and the District of Columbia. Within a 20-mile radius of Flatwoods numerous persons saw what they described variously as shooting stars, flying saucers, and aircraft in distress. Evidently these objects were different from the one seen in Flatwoods, although some of their courses could be mapped for some distance, and, if some imagination were called into play, one of them could be traced to Flatwoods.

Sanderson said he could trace the flight of the so-called meteorite seen at Flatwoods from Baltimore, Maryland, to Charleston, West Virginia, during which time it passed over Flatwoods in a curving route.

A. M. Jordan is no longer concerned with strange fiery objects that pass, out of place and reason, over his house. He died one year ago. But while still living he had seen the object which later landed on the hilltop, and was able to describe it in a matter-of-fact manner.

It was difficult for him to describe such a thing when I talked with him. For he had read no science fiction. Nor had he heard of flying saucers, nor *Fate* magazine. His reading material was restricted to newspapers and the Bible.

As he was sitting on the porch the thing had come over the horizon from the southeast. He did not look up until it had come into his view overhead and flashed in a south-westerly direction toward the hill opposite him. It was an elongated object, he said. The top of it was a light shade of a red, and the bottom bright red. From the rear shot red balls of fire. At the time he thought it was a jet plane, though he saw no wings. He did not see the nose of the object clearly. It proceeded across the sky, halted suddenly, then seemed to fall rapidly toward the hilltop.

While Jordan was pondering what he had seen, Braxton County Sheriff Robert Carr, in Sutton, received a frantic telephone call. A piper cub plane, an excited hitchhiker was reporting, had crashed into a hillside near Frametown and was burning. He had seen it from a car in which he had received a ride and had been driven to the first available telephone to report the accident.

Sheriff Carr and a deputy rushed the seventeen miles to the

19

scene, but could find no trace of the burning plane. He could find no one who had witnessed the supposed crash. The sheriff did not cross the river between the road and hillside to investigate, for he felt sure nothing had happened, since no smoke was visible. By the time he had returned to Sutton the nearby excitement about the "monster" was the talk of the town, so he drove on to answer the call received while he was at Frametown.

Anywhere from one to one and one-half hours after the appearance of the "monster" Sheriff Carr climbed the hill to investigate.

But no monster.

He could find no trace of it.

Had anyone, I asked myself, investigated earlier? For I wished to establish just when, and how, if possible, the "monster" had left.

I found that two persons, Junior Edward (about 18), who lived near the hill, and Joey Martin (about 20) were the first known investigators. They had been on the hilltop half an hour after the weird occurrence.

What, I asked them almost breathlessly, did they see. They shook their heads. They had seen, heard or smelled nothing.

Max Lockhart, a Flatwoods appliance dealer, drove his pickup truck up the narrow road to the scene about an hour after it happened, and before the sheriff arrived. Neither he nor the people with him could find any evidence of the elusive "monster."

That the "monster" could have left the scene any less spectacularly than it arrived seemed illogical. Yet nobody had seen it leave, and it had only 30 minutes to make its exit. What were we dealing with? A flying saucer that could make itself invisible?

Or a demon that had sunk into the ground, finding some dark niche in the bowels of the earth, where one science fiction writer thought lay the abode of the unlucky citizens of Atlantis, who had missed the last rocket to the stars when the chosen were evacuated to the cold blackness of space? Or more likely it was a hoax! But how a hoax? Someone might rig up a monster on the hilltop and persuade some gullible kids to come up and get scared at it. But how could this prankster arrange for a meteoric display to accompany it? The coincidence of the two events surely ruled that out.

I was less skeptical after talking to the Nunley boy, one of the eyewitnesses, and the observer nearest the "monster" when it was discovered. He tells the story without emotion, a story devoid of holes. If I can tell it as he did I'm sure you'll believe every word of it. As I did.

Neil Nunley is unspoiled by sophistication. He talks with the honest accent of West Virginia farm people, caught half-way between their staccato-voiced neighbors to the north, and the sleepier drawl of the south. He had read no science fiction, though in school the year before a teacher had read the class something (probably an account of a saucer sighting) from a "true magazine—but if it was true, you couldn't hardly believe it."

He and some other youths were at a nearby playground when they saw the strange object flash across the sky.

The boys were unanimous in disagreeing with Jordan about its color and shape. They said it looked like "a silver dollar going through the sky," and that it was not elongated. A trail of fire did shoot out behind it, however. The object was flying low, just above the hilltop over which it hovered, and "looked like a door falling down flatwise."

After it fell they could still see the light at the hilltop.

Overwhelming curiosity overtook them, so they hurriedly gathered a party, ran up the railroad track toward the foot of the
hill. They stopped at Mrs. May's house to get a flashlight, for
it was then almost dark. The two May children described the
object to their mother, who didn't believe them until she went
to the porch and saw the light, pulsing from dim to bright, on
the hill. She agreed to go with them, and Lemon led the party.

Motivation for the investigation was not to discover the terror that awaited them. There was little fear; it was mainly a
lark. They thought it was surely a meteorite and they might
see what it looked like.

Even when they encountered a strange mist near the hilltop, now smelling faintly like some kind of gas, they were
not greatly perturbed. They had no idea what they were running
onto.

Just at the hilltop there is a fence from which the gate has
rotted away. This gateway is a vantage point from which can
be seen the entire limits of the happening, none of which are
more than 100 feet away.

It was here the Lemon boy shrieked with terror, fell backward. The entire party fled.

"It looked worse than Frankenstein," Mrs. May said later.
"As long as I live I'll wish I had never seen it."

II

Flatwoods, West Virginia

I have carefully investigated the hilltop where seven people may have seen something out of space, and I have taken measurements. Whatever they saw was viewed from a short distance.

Nunley, from whose tape-recorded account I am taking much of this narrative, noticed the thing when he and Lemon, leading the party, had just stepped through the old gateway. Events described here must have taken place in a matter of seconds. Nunley, however, was able to relate the sequence with apparent accuracy.

The first thing they saw was a huge globular mass down

over the other side of the hilltop, to their right, about 50 feet away. "It was just like a big ball of fire," Nunley said, which seemed to dim and brighten at regular intervals. He didn't know how large it was; some of the others said it was "big as a house." It is not clear whether a complete sphere was seen, or a hemisphere, resting on the ground.

Nunley heard no noise. Others said it made a low thumping or beating sound, "like someone hitting on canvas," and there was another noise, half-way between a hiss and the noise made by a jet plane.

It must be pointed out that the time you consume in reading these descriptions bears no relation to the length of the experience itself. You can see many things in one second, things you might need an hour to describe. I make this comment so that you will not assume a period of observation longer than the facts indicate.

Not everyone saw the globular shape. This can be understood when one considers that the others were behind Nunley and Lemon, and that their positions might not have afforded them a view down over the hillside. And what they next saw might have been so terrifying it eradicated memory of the globe.

Distracted by the globular mass Nunley did not see a huge figure standing to their left. Lemon said he thought he saw animal eyes in the tree and flashed his light on them.

Fifteen feet away, towering over their heads, was a vast shape something like a man. The face, everyone agreed, was round, and blood red. No one noticed a nose or mouth, only eyes, or eye-like openings, from which projected "greenish-orange" beams of light. These light beams pierced through the haze pervading the scene. In the excitement some of the group thought the beams of light were focused upon them, but Nunley was specific that they were not. "They went out over our heads."

Around the red "face" and reaching upward to a point was a dark, hood-like shape. The body was seen only from the "head" down to the "waist." It appeared dark and colorless to Nunley, though some said it was green, and one child drew a picture with an outline of fire. Mrs. May said it lighted up when the flashlight beam touched it as if there were some source of illumination inside it. She also saw clothing-like folds around the body, and terrible claws. No one is sure whether the shape rested on the ground or was floating.

The "monster" could not have been more than fifteen feet tall, for it was under the overhanging limb of a tree, and the limb was of that height.

Originally the group said the strange, nauseous odor resembled burning metal, or burning sulphur. Under questioning none could remember having encountered anything similar. It was finally described only basically, as sickening, irritating to the throat and nasal passages. "It seemed to grip you in the throat and suffocate you."

Nunley was definite about the thing's movement, although other accounts conflicted. All said it was moving toward them, but according to Nunley it was describing an arc, coming toward them, but circling at the same time. His description indicated the "monster" was following a circular path which would take it back to the globe.

I asked him to walk around the room where he was being interviewed and to imitate the movement.

That was impossible, he said.

"I couldn't move as it did. It just moved. It didn't walk. It moved evenly; it didn't jump."

He was partly commenting on other reports which had the

"monster" bobbing up and down, jumping toward the witnesses.

But it must be remembered that all these details were observed within one or a few more seconds. The party didn't know how long they looked. According to Nunley it was "a very short time. We just got a good look at it and left."

"Left" here is an understatement, for the retreat was swift and disordered. No one bothered to open the gate of another fence they encountered on their return to the house.

The dog had shown no greater bravery.

They found it crouched under the porch, trembling and whining.

That a dog will take on the personalities of those around it is an observation of many, particularly among those who like to psychoanalyze animals—and people. Maybe the dog saw nothing, its great fright being motivated by the sensation of fear among the company it was with. Or maybe, as some think, animals, particularly dogs and cats, are somehow more aware of the unknown, and more sensitive to it. Some think they can see ghosts when we cannot. If there be ghosts.

I have heard the legend that there was once war on the Moon, and that the dogs and cats who lived there were banished and put down, to live on Earth. Here on Earth they still have memory of that great strife, and only superficially hold truce. And when the moon is full, and the night is warm, the dog still laments its long lost heritage with a fitful howl. Maybe it is the canine who has called the saucers down upon us.

But that is a fairy tale and a digression. If there be such things as fairies and tales and realities.

But of the "monster" the reader will think of many questions he would like to ask the witnesses. I, too, wanted to know many things. If Lemon had dropped the flashlight, as he claimed, how did they get an apparently longer look at the "monster"? Nunley said light from the globe illuminated the figure. Others said it was lighted of some source within itself. Contradictions were minor. All agreed on certain basic data I have reported, and I have noted where the stories did not agree.

I next turned to what appeared to be another very important source of information, and a vital link between the witnesses' stories and the happening. An owner of a certain funeral home in Sutton, had arrived during the first excitement, reportedly had administered first aid to some of the seven.

Here would be someone who could relate some of the first faltering descriptions these people gave, before they had any opportunity to compare experiences.

At the funeral home, while I waited for the owner's return, another man, who had stopped into the office, told me he had seen a meteorite, at seven on the same night, shoot across the sky in the direction of Flatwoods, but his story was interrupted by the appearance of the man for whom I had been waiting.

I asked him about his having treated the witnesses.

"I was in church that night," he told me, dismissing me hastily.

I know of no churches in the vicinity which held services on Friday, Sept. 12. Throughout my investigation I found an incredulous attitude on the part of nearby residents. Many did not want their names mentioned in such a connection.

"The Democrats," one man joked, "stole the state capitol dome in Charleston, and were flying it through the air to Washington. Over Weston, Rush D. Holt took a pot shot at it and knocked off one of those 'things.'" (Holt was a Republican gubernatorial candidate, was then trying to upset the Democratic majority in the state government.)

A. Lee Stewart, Jr., co-editor of *The Braxton Democrat*, was the first outside observer, in order of appearance on the scene, to offer helpful information. He arrived about half an hour after the incident.

He found some of the seven receiving first aid. Most of them appeared too greatly terrified to talk coherently. Hearing the fragmentary story, he finally was able to persuade Lemon to accompany him to the hilltop. At the moment he was skeptical, he said.

Like other investigators, he saw or heard nothing. Neither did he smell the gas which shortly before had been suffocating. But knowing that some gases settle rapidly, he bent to the ground where he could smell the same pungent odor the others described. He too said it was irritating, and constricted nasal and throat passages. Although a veteran of the Air Force, where he had encountered gases used in warfare, he had never smelled anything like it before.

To snuff for the scent at ground level had not occurred to the other investigators.

Returning at seven the following morning, before anyone else visited the hilltop in daylight, he was amazed to find evidence which backed up the story he was hesitating to report in *The Democrat*.

About ten feet apart, in the tall grass, were skid marks!

These marks proceeded from the tree where the "monster" was "standing" to the location of the globe. It was if some huge personage were on skis and had slid down the hill. But the summer skier surely was light in weight, for the "skis" had not indented the ground; they had only ridden down the tall grass, and tossed a few small stones aside. Where the globe had rested, a huge area of grass appeared to have been crushed down.

Unbelieving residents of Flatwoods gave me explanations of these marks. I checked the theory my acquaintance had earlier presented. Brooks Fisher, who owned the farm, had, he said, harvested hay at the location, and had used a tractor. Fisher had done just that, a telephone call disclosed, but he had used no tractor nor other farming implement where the marks were seen. That part of the farm, Fisher said, was too rough and steep for a tractor.

Others said Max Lockhart, an old friend of mine from high school days, had made the marks when he drove up the hill to investigate. I telephoned him.

He and some friends had driven up the hill, he confirmed, had been where the "monster" was seen, but they were not down over the hill, obviously too steep for a pickup truck.

There was foxfire on the tree, or the witnesses had seen a buck deer under it, people said. I went over the location after dark. There was no foxfire. Stewart, who hunts deer with bow and arrow, emphatically asserted that deer would be extremely unlikely at the location.

Without the interviews with the children, particularly Nunley, I would have been far more incredulous of the affair. When Mrs. May returned from New York, along with Lemon, I went to her house. By that time the story had taken on additional dimensions. Her account was far more terrifying than the one I have reported here. She had returned to the hill the next day and got grease on her beautician's uniform—a strange deposit which defied the washer. In New York she had talked to scientists who had convinced her the "monster" was a rocket ship.

But she was hesitant to give me her complete viewpoint of the experience. Someone "from the government" had asked her not to give out information to anybody, and a lawyer had advised her the story might be worth considerable money if she found the right market. Her father warned me I shouldn't "write up anything about it."

I had another opportunity to visit her home, a few weeks later. She wasn't there, but her father told me Mrs. May had received a letter from the government, which explained all the phenomena, and advised that a report was to be released to the public that week, after which date she could talk more freely about it. However, since the release date had passed, he said he was free to tell me that the "monster" was a government rocket ship, propelled by an ammonia-like hydrazine, and nitric acid.

I could hardly wait to look up editor Stewart, who, I was told, could give me details on the government report.

Stewart chuckled as he held up an 8 x 10 photo, attached to a publicity release from *Collier's* magazine. The issue of October 18 was to contain the story of how a moon rocket would be constructed in the future, and the photo was the art work which was to appear on the cover. The release date for the press was during that week, he explained. He had shown the picture to the May family because there was some resemblance between the rocket ship art work and the descriptions of the "monster." The release went on to explain how the ship could be propelled by ammonia-like hydrazine and nitric acid.

There were only wild rumors of governmental investigation. If the Air Force was interested, their concern was a well-kept secret.

I had worked three days running down leads the story involved. From a journalistic point of view the story would read better as an expose, and if it were a hoax, that was the fate it deserved. But I could neither find important holes in the evidence, nor break down the stories of the participants.

I often puzzle, however, over one account I drove 50 miles to obtain. It was said that Bailey Frame, of Birch River, who had been on the scene, had witnessed a rocket ship take off from the hill. I encountered him in a tavern at Birch River, where he hastily denied most of the report, but did say he had seen a strange object in the sky after the incident.

It was a large orange ball, he said, flattened on top, from which jets or streams of fire shot out and down around the sides. It circled around the sky, and was seen from a small valley at Flatwoods, near the hilltop, where he had driven half an hour after hearing about the matter. After circling for about 15 minutes it suddenly left, at great speed, toward the Sutton airport.

As surely as the "monster" came on wings of fire, so rapidly it had flashed away. Here, I thought, was the important link—the exit of the creature.

Frame said he'd be glad to meet me at a restaurant that evening, drive to Flatwoods with me, and take me to the exact spot where he was standing when he saw the thing.

He didn't show up.

I would like to clear something else up—if I were only able. On a nearby hill, in complete view of that fateful hilltop that enmeshed me in the saucer mystery, lives G. D. Hoard, an elderly farmer. Reports had it that Hoard had told an amazing story about seeing the entire incident, but editor Stewart said he shut up like a clam when he tried to interview him.

When I talk to many people I lead off by telling them I "was raised on a farm," which, incidentally, is true. That seems to disarm them, and country people soon lose their mistrust of "city folks."

Hoard said he'd be glad to tell me everything he had seen. At about seven P.M. he had been in his front yard feeding his chickens. His attention was drawn to a fiery object coming over the horizon, though in a slightly different direction than others reported. It did not land, but went on across the sky.

"It went over the Bailey Fisher cistern and as it was about here (and he pointed to a location roughly in line with his house) a piece of fire broke off it." As it neared the other horizon, toward the Sutton airport, "it exploded and went out."

Now if this were the same object, one would believe it didn't land at all. And if Hoard were in his yard at the time when the "monster" appeared, why did he not see the amazing occurrence on the nearby hilltop, easily within his view?

One person, who also investigated, feels that Hoard saw much more than he wishes to relate, that he does not want publicity.

I would really like to know.

❋ ❋ ❋ ❋ ❋

In completing my investigation I went to Frametown with Sanderson and his assistant. We slashed our way up the brushy hillside with machetes, hoping to find evidence of the mysterious "plane crash" the hitchhiker had reported.

We spent the entire afternoon canvassing the hills. Now and

then we thought we saw tree limbs broken off unnaturally, but really we found nothing concrete.

The hitchhiker had not been afforded a clear view of the burning object. A piper cub was the first thing that came to his mind, he said, and he didn't know what it was. In interviewing other people who saw what most of them termed "meteorites," I found most of them thought these crashed into nearby hills.

Probably no one may ever know exactly what seven people saw on a West Virginia hilltop. The following, however, is in my opinion definite:

(1) Widespread aerial phenomena, generally interpreted as meteorites, were observed at approximately the same time over a wide area.

(2) The seven witnesses *did* see *something* that was terrifying and unfamiliar, something rather similar to that which they described.

It is the interpretation of these points that is difficult.

Because of the widespread talk of and belief in flying saucers, I was inclined to connect the incident with that vast mystery. The appearance of the thing before it presumably landed was similar to many so-called flying saucers, though it presented different aspects to different viewers. The aerial object seen by Mr. Jordan and the children did not behave like a meteorite.

If saucerian in nature, why did it land? Was it in mechanical difficulty? Or did its pilot wish to make observations?

The strange figure evidently was connected with the globular object. The spot where it was viewed was a vantage point, from which the surrounding countryside could be observed, if some interplanetary or intergalactic visitors were interested in sightseeing.

Why and how did it leave so suddenly?

Could it have been a robot, controlled mechanically? Its movements and the skid marks could indicate such to someone who might use science fiction or scientific conjecture as a standard. Or was it a man, or a "thing," in a space suit? It is possible that on some fantastic planet some fantastic being is writing a book on some sort of marvelous typewriter. Typewriters there are so far advanced in development they have only to be spoken into. They click out words in wild staccato while a metallic hand inserts fresh pages. It is a horror study. In super-purple words the author tells how he made a forced landing, and was attacked by seven strange bipeds of configuration too terrible to describe.

One of them shot at him with a ray.

* * * * *

Three years have passed since some people were almost scared out of their wits in Flatwoods. Passing there recently I ran across the Nunley boy walking along the road. He didn't seem to be interested in talking further about the "monster," but was greatly concerned about a plane crash that had occurred at a nearby airport. We drove to the airport, looked at the wrecked plane, while I tried to get back on the subject.

"You weren't pulling my leg, were you," I asked him, and again he assured me he was not.

"I just don't know what it was, but I saw it."

The excitement has about died down, but West Virginians in the reach of radio singer Cindy Coy still love to hear the inevitable ballad composed by announcer Don Lamb.

To the lonesome chords of the steel guitar Cindy sings, over and over, for enthusiastic listeners:

"THE PHANTOM OF FLATWOODS"
(Sing to tune of "Sweet Betsy From Pike")

One evenin' in Flatwoods, a mother and her boys
Saw a great light and heard a great noise.
They ran to the hilltop, didn't know what they feared,
It was there in the dark that the Phantom appeared.

(CHORUS)

Oh, Phantom of Flatwoods, from Moon or from Mars
Maybe from God and not from the stars,
Please tell us why you fly o'er our trees
The end of the world or an omen of peace?

The size of the phantom was a sight to behold,
Green eyes and red face, so the story was told.
It floated in air with fingers of flame.
It was gone with a hiss just as quick as it came.

(CHORUS)

The people were frightened and started to pray
They were living in hopes of another new day,
There's no end to this story, except just to say
This world will go on for it's written that way.

(CHORUS)

Brush Creek, California

You are John Q. Black.

You stand there near the sandbar, surrounded by 200 people, waiting for a flying saucer to return.

You hope it will so you can prove to the world you aren't a liar.

But there is no flying saucer, and there is no little man, dipping water from the junction of Jordan and Marble Creeks. Dipping water in a bucket that is like no bucket on the face of this Earth.

When the saucer doesn't show up, most of the people are nice about it. They disperse, leaving you to wonder.

Altogether you have seen the thing seven times; four times you saw it in the air; it wasn't until you saw it taking off from under your very nose you began giving much thought to it.

But on July 20, 1953, you came face to face with something so unusual, yet something so real, that no one, not even yourself, can convince you the story you tell is a falsehood.

Such was the story that was coming out of Brush Creek, California. Reporters and columnists had a field day relating how a man from space had alighted from a flying saucer and got a bucket of water from the creek. Two titanium miners had witnessed the odd events on two separate occasions and had applied for permission to shoot at the saucer the next time it landed.

And here I was again, reading the paper (probably as it lay under my breakfast dishes, though I don't now remember). Ever since investigating the incident in Flatwoods, West Virginia, I had been seeing more and more flying saucer accounts and stories of other unusual events in my morning paper. Maybe more saucer stories were being published, though I suspect I found them because I was looking for them.

I think most people in show business, particularly motion picture exhibition, succumb to a particular habit with pathological consequences. Each morning they sit down at the breakfast table with a newspaper, opened first to the entertainment page. Their primary concern, and worry, is usually what pictures the competition is showing.

It is a tremulously exciting event, as you fearfully cast your eyes onto the page, expecting the worst. This is particularly true when the exhibitor, as I do, prepares newspaper advertising layouts for theatres. In that case, catastrophic typographical errors are expected, and they usually occur.

Take the time I had a bosomy shot of Joan Crawford in my ad. I had written the copy, to be set directly above, as "TWO BIG HITS." The "TWO BIG" part of the catchline was printed correctly. That the rest of the phrase, changed greatly in meaning by one wrong letter, evinced smiles among my colleagues and acquaintances is an understatement.

But there is something about flying saucers and the prospect of space travel that almost takes over a person's entire life once he gets the "bug." I'm afraid that is what happened to me.

I would write a book about flying saucers and psychology if I were a psychologist. If you can explain psychology you can explain saucers—or a great percentage of them. But I can't even psychoanalyze myself.

Anyhow, by late 1953 I was becoming what a great many people interested in saucers term a "saucer addict." Somehow I wanted to find out just what they really were, where they came from, and, more important, *why* they were here.

My addiction was becoming serious, for instead of first gazing fearfully at the entertainment page, I was scanning through the news columns for saucer items.

The papers seemed to be full of the stuff.

A Shiloh, Ohio, man watched a 70-second dogfight between two flying disks. Wilgus A. Patton was driving when he saw two "shining things" whirling around each other. He pointed out the objects to his wife and children, parked his auto off the road. "The two things looked like tadpoles at first glance. They were tremendously large, and appeared to be flying at about 1,000 feet and about three miles away from us." The objects were diving at each other. They headed north suddenly and disappeared "in a flash."

A Cleveland, Ohio, man saw "a huge white-rimmed saucer, bigger than a house, flying through the northern sky," on August 13, 1953. George Popovic and his wife watched it from their front yard for two minutes about two A.M. After it disappeared they saw something that looked like two misty clouds in the sky, also very white.

Policemen in the San Francisco area saw what looked like a "light bulb" maneuvering in the sky. Four United States airmen in Korea watched a small, white, delta-shaped object flying at about 80 miles per hour over Communist territory on the western front. First Lieutenant Edward Balocco chased a silvery object over Washington, North Carolina. It appeared at first to be an airplane, with red lights. Soon he observed it was traveling too fast for conventional aircraft. He chased it at more than 500 miles per hour, but was unable to catch up with it.

And skywatchers' logs were filled with objects which didn't behave like airplanes.

Air Force investigators were already issuing their Press Bulletins about saucers, had already evolved a classic form of doubletalk, and the even more classic "Fact Sheet."

Project Saucer, the organization set up to investigate the snowballing disk reports, had been officially abandoned, but investigators were still studying the problem, according to Lieutenant Robert M. Olsson, of Wright Patterson Air Force Base.

All but 14 per cent of the sightings turned in to them could be explained, Olsson stated, as atmospheric phenomena, conventional objects such as balloons, and so on. The remaining 14 per cent could also be explained, Lieutenant Olsson felt, if the Air Force had the proper data. A new type of camera, utilizing a diffraction grating, would soon be put into use, and this special attachment would afford a spectroscopic analysis of any objects sighted. provided they had incandescent exhaust trails.

The Air Force reviewed one unsolved sighting near Albuquerque, New Mexico, which occurred on January 26, 1953. Several persons saw a bright red light, hanging low on the horizon, for about 40 minutes. Radar picked up a "blip" corresponding to the location of the visual sighting, and investigators didn't yet know just what the thing could have been, though they felt certain it was caused by "atmospheric conditions." Such gaseous gyrations of the elements could play tricks even on radar, they said, since beams were often reflected to Earth by temperature inversions. Under such conditions a truck traveling along a highway might be picked up by radar as an object flashing through the sky at 2,000 miles an hour!

Yet the Air Force was still zealously chasing flying trailer trucks and was sure, at least, of one thing:

"The Air Force has stated in the past, and reaffirms at the present time," plodded on the August 28, 1953, Fact Sheet, "that these unidentified aerial phenomena are not a secret weapon, missile or aircraft, developed by the United States. None of the three military departments nor any other agency in the government is conducting experiments, classified or otherwise, with flying objects which could be a basis for the reported phenomena."

Nor did investigators fear similar objects developed by other countries, nor, of course, other planets.

Earlier that year a temperature inversion had swooshed down and landed in Mrs. Walker's pecan tree. The inversion looked just like a man, though it was odd that he had a pair of big black wings, and flew over the house of Mrs. Hilda Walker, of Houston, Texas, "like a white flash of a torpedo-shaped object."

The bat man, or whatever he was, was seen to alight in the tree. When Mrs. Walker and two other persons looked up they saw "the figure of a man with wings like a bat. He was dressed in gray or black tight-fitting clothes." After perching in the tree half a minute the halo surrounding him began to fade and the strange figure disappeared.

The bat man was about six and a half feet tall, and all this had happened on June 18, at 2:30 A.M. Witnesses besides Mrs. Walker, a housewife, age 23, were Howard Phillips, tool plant inspector, 33; 14-year-old Judy Meyers.

No one saw the bat man's saucer, though saucer addicts presumed he had arrived in one. Bird men, if new to saucer-dom, were not new to Washington, according to some saucer enthusiasts, who often felt there were a great many parrots in the Pentagon.

Other strange things were happening. Although the Air Force wasn't concerned with poltergeists, one of these mischievous spirits was raising hell in Alabama, at Nathan Irving's farm home near Bessemer, in July. An oil heater and a china cabinet jumped around. Several tables and chairs jumped off the floor and fell over. All this was accompanied by a barrage of rocks falling from the roof and bricks falling from places where bricks ought not to be. Besides all this excitement, knives, according to Irving, "jumped from the dishpan to the floor."

Otherwise things were normal. Arthur Godfrey went back on the air, the Russians exploded a hydrogen bomb, and Prof. Alfred E. Kinsey revealed that women, too, were not to be trusted too far outside the house.

Since I had got mixed up with the Flatwoods "monster" I had also become enmeshed with a lot of people interested in the same thing. Letters poured in from all over the United States and the world, partly because of my *Fate* magazine article, but mainly because I evolved the idea of printing all of the saucer news I received in a quarterly publication which I titled *The Saucerian*.

The Saucerian, I learned, was the only publication of its type in circulation which attempted to give a full coverage to saucer sightings. The first issue had been very crude, run off on an office spirit duplicator. In looking back over that initial attempt to inform the public about saucers, I find one statement in particular, part of the editorial, that makes a lot of sense and even today is not out of date:

"The writer has definite beliefs and ideas about the saucers as follows:

"(1) The saucers are real, do exist, and have been seen by hundreds of reliable people (the editor has never seen one).

"(2) The saucers are alien to the known part of our world or to the Earth entirely.

"(3) The saucers are not secret government developments, Russian spies, or the planet Venus.

"(4) Although a great many saucers can be explained away as misinterpretation of natural phenomena, mass hysteria, mirages, etc., such cannot account for 100% of recorded sightings."

In *The Saucerian*, I told my readers, I hoped to contribute to the answer. The answer to an important question: *"What are they?"*

* * * * *

But back to the start of this chapter. Back to you and John Q. Black, and the little man and the bucket of water.

Black and his partner, John J. Van Allen, operated titanium diggings near Brush Creek, in Butte County, California. One day, according to newspaper stories reaching *The Saucerian* from some of the many unofficial civilian investigators who were helping me, Black saw a little man dipping a bucket of water from Marble Creek. He automatically assumed it was a child, but soon changed his mind when he saw the figure climb into a saucer-shaped contraption and take off.

The newspapers generally pooh-poohed the account, though they did note that the village storekeeper averred the miners were "not drinking men."

To me the story somehow smacked of truth, and I felt I should try and get to the bottom of it. Paul Spade, an amateur astronomer of California, who had volunteered his services to saucer investigation in his area, also volunteered to go to Brush Creek and look into the matter.

Spade made what I considered an objective investigation, reported that the story was evidently not a hoax after all.

Altogether, Spade found, there had been seven sightings of the saucer-shaped craft. Four times it was seen in the air, apparently not too close to the ground, for the miners had not been sufficiently impressed to set down those four dates.

But on April 20 the saucer was bolder. They saw it at a distance of about a quarter of a mile, passing soundlessly against a hillside from north to south.

Van Allen had seen it twice in the air, but the close appearances were witnessed by Black alone. Evidently little thought was given to the goings-on until May 20 at 6:30 P.M. On that date Black came over the top of a rock about ten feet from the junction of Jordan and Marble Creeks, saw the saucer hovering above the sandbar about 150 feet away. Then it took off, flying east down the creek with a hissing noise. It was from this and the following closer view that Black was able to estimate the size and describe the shape accurately, although the machine seen earlier in the air appeared identical as far as he could tell.

On May 20 someone or something had built a campfire, because they found coals floating in the creek and could see where the fire had been built on a rock. This evidently is the basis for one newspaper story which had the saucer starting a brush fire when it took off. Black found small five-inch footprints at the site, and on one occasion his compass had spun around wildly, although he had seen no disk at that particular time.

But it was only on June 20 that Black saw any creature connected with the saucer, the craft at rest on the ground, and the bucket-of-water episode.

On that date Black came face to face with something from outside, something or someone on a prosaic errand that would titillate the fancy of a nation.

Black was in the woods when he looked at the junction of the two creeks and saw a small person bent down at the water. It looked like a boy fishing, so he paid no attention. Later, when he was further down the creek, he saw the person again, now only about 40 feet away, dipping water in a bucket. Then he saw the saucer, and knew that if this was a fisherman his vacation had taken him many miles from home.

And he had never seen a fisherman dressed like this one.

Paul Spade spent four days camping with the miners in order to win their trust and obtain the full story. Included in their complete accounts of the several incidents with the saucer was a detailed description of the saucerman:

The little man wore green trousers, a jacket and a tie. His shoes were particularly strange in that they seemed to be so remarkably flexible. Although they were distinctly recognizable as shoes, they seemed almost to be a part of the man's feet. The outfit was topped off with a green cap over black hair.

He looked like a normal person except for the small stature and somewhat odd dress. The walk was stiff, as if his muscles were cramped. He was broad-shouldered, appeared to be strong, and was rather good-looking—for a saucerman. He was very pale. As Black put it, "He looked like someone who had never been out in the sun much."

Black was greatly interested in the activity of the little man, who was dipping a bucket of water from the creek. The bucket had a flat round bottom and a bail, but Black had never seen a bucket quite like it. The sides flared out like the segments of a cone. It looked like aluminum, or some other shiny metal.

As he crept closer to get a better look, he stepped on a dry stick. The little man heard the noise, looked up and down the creek, but apparently didn't see Black, obscured by trees and bushes. He hurried to the saucer standing nearby, got into the thing and was off for those elusive climes from which he had somehow come.

The best way Black could describe the saucer was that it looked like two large soup plates fastened together, forming a convex shape. It was a shiny metallic color, and no rivets were visible. He estimated the size as about eight feet in diameter. It was approximately four and a half feet thick at the center. It was resting on a cylinder, a pipe-like understructure from which hand-holds jutted at intervals, like the spikes on a telephone pole.

There was a window in the side of the saucer, but it afforded no view of the interior. Black supposed it was a window; it looked like one. There was no observation dome. There was no smell of gas or any other substance.

The little man climbed up the pipe-like understructure. His feet, in their oddly flexible shoes, curled around each spike. He climbed until all of his body above the knees had vanished through an opening in the base of the saucer, then seemed to sit down and lift up his legs. The craft rocked as he got in, the base was drawn up into the body, and the saucer hovered in the air for a few seconds, then took off at a 45° angle with a hissing sound.

No visible means of propulsion could be observed. On one occasion (it is not stated whether on June 20 or May 20) the efficient control of the machine was evident as it was rising through some trees, without room to clear the tops. It slipped sideways between them until it gained altitude. On one occasion Black waved his hat at the saucer in the air, and it seemed to reply by wobbling a little.

The world first heard the story when sheriff's captain Fred Preston was in the Brush Creek area on June 24, investigating a burglary case, and ran across Black. According to newspaper reports, Black asked him if he had been hearing any reports on flying saucers. When the sheriff said he hadn't, Black replied, "Well, I saw one," and then told of the incidents.

Neither Black nor Van Allen had any intention of shooting at the visitor. Newspapers picked up that angle after Black jokingly asked the sheriff if it were "open season on space men."

* * * * *

Maybe it was the same saucer, maybe people were just looking for them, but the Brush Creek incident touched off a wave of saucer reports in the surrounding territory.

On July 13 Mrs. Ethel G. Carson saw a disk darting through the skies at four A.M. traveling toward the Cohasset area. It was emitting sparks, "just like fireworks." Mr. and Mrs. Allan Rice, of Pleasant Valley, whom she was visiting, also saw it. They said it was "about a quarter as big as a full moon," and "seemed to be hanging right over the foothills."

On July 15 Mrs. Joyce Battrell, of nearby Chico, saw a silver-colored disk-shaped object hovering in the air about one-fourth of a mile from her house. She was standing on the front porch at about seven in the evening when she noticed the object hanging in space above an almond orchard across from her house. It then began to revolve slowly and move away. She summoned a neighbor, Mrs. E. H. Burnight, but when the latter came the object had moved off in a northwesterly direction until it was only a speck in the sky. Don Burnight, the neighbor's 24-year-old son, thought it was an airplane, but the women said there was no motor noise. Mrs. Battrell drew a sketch which resembled the saucer seen at Brush Creek.

Another woman, who refused to give her name to reporters, said she was working in the garden of her Lindo Way home when she spotted a "real shiny" object practically standing still in the sky. She had talked with Mrs. Battrell after reading of her sighting in the papers and they found they both had been looking in the same direction.

On July 16 Mrs. Hannah Stone, of Chico, saw a silver-colored object in the sky, which "veered like it was going over the city, then it turned sharply toward the north and rose rapidly until it went out of sight. It was round, looked something like a large transparent baseball. It was approaching Chico from the west, almost lazily at first. Then it turned north-ward and speeded up."

On July 21 Mr. and Mrs. Joe Carlos, of Chico, saw a "bright object, just like a flying saucer," at six P.M. while fishing on the Feather River near Oroville. The object went toward Oroville. On August 10 Mrs. Susan Perdue, of Oroville, saw five saucers with green lights, zooming overhead toward the west at high speed. They flew at low altitude, making no sound.

On August 16 J. R. Bowling, of Chico, saw four flashes of light between half-past two and three o'clock in the afternoon while fishing on the Feather River, about four miles from Brush Creek. These looked like they might be magnesium flares— "That's what they reminded me of. They were a kind of bluish green in color. The first one appeared round and then flat on the edges. It was going too rapidly to attempt a description. The others were just split-second flashes of light."

These recent happenings hold no monopoly on strange goings-on in the area. A rain of small fishes fell from a cloudless sky in Chico on August 20, 1878, covering several acres. On the night of March 5, 1885, a large object weighing several tons and of a very hard material fell from the sky near the town. In the early part of 1922 a series of rock showers attracted na-tionwide attention.

* * * * *

In the meantime, Black and Van Allen were figuring that, since the flying disk had shown up on April 20, May 20, and June 20, it would be likely to put in another appearance on July 20.

Paul Spade, continuing his investigation, decided to visit the

Brush Creek area four days in advance to be on hand for the event. He found the miners friendly and hospitable. They didn't seem to want publicity, but willingly gave him an account of what had happened so far. Spade camped with them, spent most of the days fishing at a vantage point from which he could see any saucer that might come visiting. But he saw nothing.

One night after he had turned in, Black came to him, asked him to go with him up the road to check on a light he saw in the canyon. They could see a glow, and the tree trunks seemed to be lighted up from all sides, not from one direction only. Spade went down into the canyon, where he was able to see a light flickering through the trees. Black also saw the light, which soon disappeared. Spade also saw searchlights in the sky that night, searchlights which did not seem to rise from ground level but to originate in the air.

Then came zero hour.

July 20 at 6:30 P.M.

All eyes centered on a tree, a focal point for the appearances, so Black said.

People had been arriving at the spot all day. More than two hundred had gathered to get a look at the elusive space visitor. The face of the man from Mars, or from wherever he had come, would be recorded for posterity to stare at. Eric Mayell and Thoreau Willat, cameramen for United Press Movietone films and the Telenews Corporation, held heavy movie cameras focused at infinity, their nervous fingers on buttons that would start the sprockets buzzing the minute the saucer appeared.

But George T. Wolfer, a Milwaukee sales executive, held a camera more appropriate to the modernity and novelty of the occasion. His converted Bolex movie camera would record the saucer in three dimensions, and in color too; the world could tell if the little man was solid. Meanwhile Black recited the background of the story into a tape recorder for Chico's radio station KXOC.

An archer had appeared with bow and blunted arrows, the only armament present. With these, he explained, the visitor could be first stunned, then captured. But he was talked out of his plans by others who felt a more friendly approach should be made.

And in case the saucerman turned out to be a thinking creature, two telepaths were there to read his mind, or to communicate with him if that were possible.

But 6:30 came and went, darkness fell, cameras grew heavy in the hands. No little man, no flying saucer, no bucket of water.

Black was asked if he expected the visitor to return.

"I do! I expect to see it sometime this summer!" He spoke as if he believed what he said.

"Have you drawn any conclusions about the space visitor?"

"No, I have not. It's too deep for me. I'm just a miner. My conscience is clear, and I have a clear record. I know that I will see it again."

And the assemblage dispersed, walking slowly away, over the rough lumber road.

* * * * *

If still unproven, the story had attracted national attention. When first reported, phone calls flooded newspaper offices and the sheriff's office. If the sheriff couldn't confirm or explain what had happened, at least he did set down a precedent for dealing with saucermen. It wasn't permissible to shoot at them, he said, but there should be some effort to capture them or to take pictures.

A Comstock, Michigan, woman exhorted Black and Van Allen to show no violence toward the visitors. Because the saucer showed up on the twentieth of each month, she believed they were moon men.

"Please tell these miners not to shoot at them," she wrote, reviewing the terrors of a war between Earth and another planet.

Another *Chico Enterprise-Record* reader, John Gray, gave freely of interplanetary advice. He believed "Whatever can be said of flying saucers they do not come from outer space.

"A fish swims because it has a muscle in its tail. Not that alone for it must have been in the element called water. Shag him, yank him out on the bank and we say of him that he flops violently. . . . The element he is in does not respond to his wiggles. In the water and with two such wiggles he is out of sight."

Aircraft, flying saucers, "such as are said to have lit to take on a pail of water, are in their element. The tail of which whirls instead of switches." But to take an aircraft out of its element, according to Gray, would be quite disastrous: "As the ship travels out of the air envelope, rockets exploding would just be a noise no one could hear, there being no air to kick back against, that would be an end of the flying. . . . The ship would fall back into the air envelope, and let's hope it got going again."

In San Francisco, California, a district enforcement officer for the Immigration and Naturalization Service provided an interesting sidelight to the Brush Creek flying saucer story, and, to my knowledge, set down the world's first interplanetary (or intergalactic) interpretation of immigration laws.

He would he said discourage any such visitors from taking sightseeing tours in the United States.

"Brush Creek is not a port of entry. Men from Mars are not citizens. Non-citizens are aliens. Aliens without visas issued by American Consulates cannot enter. There is no American Consul on Mars or anywhere else in outer space."

Such visitors would not be sent away without a hearing, according to the district officer, who further observed, "It is inconceivable, however, that the outcome could be other than an order of exclusion and deportation to point of origin, aboard whatever carrier brought them here."

He added that such deportation would be strictly "at the carrier's expense."

Meanwhile Robert Coe Gardner, flying saucer lecturer from San Francisco, was telling spellbound members of the Chico Art Club that as far as the Brush Creek episode was concerned, he believed Black and Van Allen had experienced a "psychic aberration," which "resembled a mirage."

The footnote to *The Saucerian's* investigation of the Brush Creek Story was both enigmatic and embarrassing for our on-the-spot investigator. Since the sightings were reported to have occurred on the twentieth of each month, Spade decided to be at the landing site on September 20. He was thrown into jail and told never to visit the section again! Why?

I hoped I would find the answer in Spade's report, reproduced here as he submitted it to *Saucerian* headquarters.

I arrived by Greyhound bus at Oroville in the afternoon of September 18 and caught a ride to Brush Creek on a lumber truck. At the Brush Creek store I inquired if the two miners were still in the area, but was disappointed to learn they had left suddenly. This was odd, since they told me they were not in the habit of leaving until the first storms of winter drove them out.

I then went to the mining camp eight miles up the road from Brush Creek. When I reached the miners' camp site I put my pack and canned goods in the framework for a tent they had left there, got into my sleeping bag and retired.

The next day I went to the landing site at the junction of Jordan and Marble Creeks, and took an all-day hike downstream from this point to see if I could find evidence of any new landings; but the search proved futile and I returned to my camp site. I was eating supper when I heard a car coming down the road. It was a ranger in a jeep. He stopped and gave my camp site a "fishy" look, and did not give me the friendly "howdy" I had heard so often from the lumbermen and other friendly natives of that area. So I continued eating and didn't give him more than a side glance.

He left shortly, and when I was through eating I went to a spot overlooking the landing site and sat watching it until twilight; then I returned to camp where I chanced to glance up and saw a hovering, glowing light about the size of Jupiter under 50X magnification. I hoped at first that it would land, but it began moving from its position east of me in a southerly direction, and soon passed from sight. It was light amber in color and made no audible sound. I continued watching the sky for some time, but nothing further showed up. So I retired.

I was awakened later that night by someone shining a flashlight in my face. When I opened my eyes I saw a sheriff's car with two men in it. A third was approaching me with his flashlight aimed directly at me.

He asked me if I was comfortable and when I assured him

that I was, he asked me to gather up my things and come along. I asked him what the charge was, and he said he wasn't taking me on any charge, but for my protection. He said I was in dangerous bear and cougar country and I should be armed. He also said the ranger who turned me in was afraid I might start a forest fire. I told them I didn't smoke and was eating my food out of a can and had no intention of starting a campfire. On the way to Oroville, which, by the way, is 35 miles from the place they found me, I began to wonder if perhaps they suspected me of stealing something from the mine. So I told them I had come to the area to see if the saucers came periodically on the twentieth of each month, as the miners had claimed.

They asked me if I had seen any saucers while I was up there, and I told them about the sighting just before they had arrived. I also told them I had at one time belonged to a saucer research group in San Diego. When we reached Oroville it was midnight and they asked me where I lived, the names of my relatives, etc.

They put me in a solitary cell in the Butte County jail. They didn't provide me with a spoon at breakfast the next morning, so I began eating with a piece of bread. When one of the attendants came down the corridor I asked him for a spoon. He slid one to me under the door, across the dirty floor. A little later I noticed there was a service bell, so I rang it in the hope they would tell me the charge on which I was being held, and how long they intended to keep me in jail. When someone came, I asked him what the charge was, and he smiled and said, "Don't you know?"

I asked him if my relatives had been notified and he said they had, which I found later to be untrue. That afternoon the sheriff who brought me in came in and told me he was going to release me but I couldn't return to the mountains. I told him I was not fully prepared to give the idea up and still wished to return. He then asked me if I had ever been in a mental hospital. I told him that I hadn't, and he said they were worried about my mental health and explained that if anything happened to me while I was in the mountains the blame would fall on the county.

From his manner of speaking I got the impression the talk about my mental health was "cooked up" to have an excuse for holding me.

He said that since I still wished to go to the mountains, I would need official permission, and he would arrange an interview with the district attorney, but in the meantime I would have to return to my cell. I asked, "Do you think it's good for a person's mental health to be kept in solitary?" So they saw that I got some company, put me in the drunk tank.

Next afternoon I was taken to the Oroville district attorney's office where I was asked to give a review of my reasons for wanting to go back to the mountains. I told them the same thing I had told the sheriff: that I had at one time belonged to a saucer research group, was assigned by a magazine to determine if a saucer would show up on the twentieth. Of course it was already September 21, but I still had hopes I might see something further, as I had on the nineteenth. The district attorney said he would give the sheriff a ring a little later to let him decide if it would be all right for me to return to the mountains. But night came and I was still in jail.

The next afternoon I was taken to an upstairs room where I was fingerprinted and photographed. Then I was taken to the court house, where I was given a paper ordering a hearing for me as a mentally ill person. The court was called to order and I was questioned by a psychiatrist, with the sheriff and district attorney as witnesses.

I was asked, among other questions, if I were sure that what I saw on September 19 was a saucer, or if it could have been car lights farther up the road. Was I positive that was what I had seen? There were also a few questions about the research group to which I had belonged. I assured them all they had to do to verify that was to call any of the group members whose names I gave them. After a few more questions the psychiatrist said he saw no grounds for a mental hearing and suggested dismissal of the case, and the judge acted accordingly.

I asked the judge if there was any law to keep me out of the Sierras. He said there was not, but advised me not to go there. When I went back to the sheriff's office to gather my belongings he came up to me and said, "I hope you don't have any hard feelings. We were doing this in your interest and for your protection."

I will always wonder if that was the case.

* * * * *

That was the Brush Creek Story, amazing, fantastic, undocumented.

Did Black actually see a flying saucer, or was he telling tall tales? Or was it an hallucination, or one of those mysterious "Menzelforms," a word coined by British researcher Richard Hughes to apply to those sightings of the type explained away by Donald H. Menzel, in his book, *Flying Saucers?*

The prosaic mission of the saucerman is almost classic in its simplicity.

A bucket of water.

There have been other reports of little men, many of which,

though more terrifying than the Brush Creek visitor, were concerned with water and streams and handfuls of earth. After
all, if the little men are real, and are visiting here, what could
be more logical than taking samples of soil and water? We will
do the same thing when we first set foot on another planet. If
they have soil. If they have water.

One thing that militates against conclusions in the saucer
mystery is the many theories that are evolved, once the investigator begins to turn the data over in his mind.

One such investigator, Barry Sheehy, in the August, 1953,
issue of *The Australian Flying Saucer Magazine,* one of the
flurry of such publications that started to come out about the
time *The Saucerian* was first issued, had a theory that might
apply to the Brush Creek affair. Sheehy believed the saucers
were coming here from Mars, where, considering all those canals,
there must be a water shortage. With the remaining water sup-
ply gradually disappearing, owing to Mars' low gravitation,
maybe the Martians were running tankers here to get a com-
modity we'd never suspect would be valuable to interplanetary
visitors!

Or maybe it was a visitor from the planet Grond, described
by the tellers of fiction? Their delicate glass cities spin between
us and the Moon; there water is a curiosity and a laboratory
child. Or was it an Esoteric One, or an envoy from the Secret
Rulers of the Earth, reporting if the time was right?

Or was it from the caverns, deep in the Earth's core, extend-
ing from the Golden Gate to the storied cities of the East, where,
it is said by Richard S. Shaver, a race of degenerate beings
plays with stim rays?

Whatever Black saw, the story sounds almost too good for
someone to think up, especially when such a story is credited

to an isolated miner, who is not likely to be at all well-read on science fiction.

As publisher of a flying saucer magazine I was daily receiving stories that were almost incompatible with reason, or the reason I had set up as a standard for reality. Were all of these people lying? Hardly, I thought. Were they having hallucinations? Some of them, maybe. Or did we have visitors from somewhere, somewhere on the outside? If we did, scientific and physical standards we had set up might not even apply to, say, a race of beings advanced thousands of years beyond us in scientific prowess and social organization. They might not even think as we did. They might have an entirely different concept of morals and ethics.

If there were an organization of people interested in the saucer mystery, so that there could be a pool of research facilities and information, maybe all of them, working together, could unravel the tenuous threads of the enigma.

If, I thought, some aggressive individual could organize such a group, the entire Flying Saucer Mystery might be cracked much more quickly than one would anticipate.

That is where Bender came in.

IV

Lemuria

It was through Albert K. Bender that I was plunged into one of the most mystifying and bizarre enigmas I have ever encountered while trying to uncover the facts about flying saucers.

Had I known how many miles I would travel, how many transcontinental telephone calls I would make, and how many nights I would sit up until the early morning hours, desperately trying to fit the strange pattern together, I probably would have dropped the entire business right there and looked for a simpler way of occupying myself in my spare time—like climbing Mt. Everest.

But I'm getting ahead of myself. I first heard Bender's name in 1952, but the path that led me to him began long before, in a college dormitory. My room mate had purchased a copy of *Amazing Stories*, then edited by Ray Palmer, and he lent it to me. In that magazine was a hair-raising and fantastic story by Richard S. Shaver, and I read it. There was no sleep for me that night. Reason and logic were against belief, and my touchstones and guides were reason, logic, professors and textbooks. Unlike many others, I never accepted the theories put forth by Shaver as true, but even to me it seemed that somewhere in the Shaver Mystery was a haunting ring of truth.

Shaver was "discovered" by Palmer. Shaver wrote about flying saucers before Kenneth Arnold saw "a chain of saucerlike things" skipping along above Mt. Rainier in 1947, and told the press about the experience, thus coining a word that will forever plague saucer research, and attaching a humorous and therefore necessarily suspicious connotation to the mystery.

Shaver said space ships were coming from other planets to visit someone here on Earth, someone that ordinary people didn't know about. A secret society that lived madly and phantasmagorically, in marvelous caverns deep under the surface of our planet.

It all started in late 1943 with a letter thrown into a waste basket because it was "crackpot," and Raymond E. Palmer diving to retrieve it. Palmer, as I have said, was editor of *Amazing Stories*, a science fiction publication of large circulation. Howard Browne was an assistant editor. Browne has achieved a kind of immortality for throwing that letter away, for it was written by Richard S. Shaver, a Pittsburgh, Pennsylvania, welder, and it contained what the writer claimed was an ancient alphabet antedating man, an alphabet called Mantong which was the phonetic key to all languages. The alphabet would still work, Shaver claimed, in English. Instead of being a modern language, the letter averred, English was closer to being the mother lode of all languages than a derivation from an ancient source.

Some people think that Browne should have clobbered Palmer then and there. For the letter was the beginning of a mystery which would catch the entire nation's imagination, would result in the receipt of thousands of letters of praise and even confirmation, but at the same time disturb a lot of people who felt dangerously close to believing Shaver's story, dangerously close to losing their reason.

"We may have the key to man's past here," Palmer exclaimed in print when he published the letter. And many readers apparently agreed. According to Palmer, the alphabet worked with an amazing exactness, increasing in accuracy as one delved farther back into time. In ancient Egyptian the alphabet allegedly proved satisfactory in 95 per cent of the instances tried.

Encouraged by seeing the letter in print Shaver sent Palmer a gratis manuscript purporting to be true. Palmer didn't believe the story, but he published it, rewriting and disguising it as fiction in order, he thought, to make it palatable to science fiction readers.

Shaver's narrative began with an account of voices coming through a welding machine. His first thought was that he had gone nuts. But he began to wonder, when the voices imparted information that could not possibly, he believed, originate in his subconscious; when they gave him scientific and engineering data far beyond his grasp and education, some of which was vouched for by reputable and amazed engineers.

Deep below the surface of the Earth, the voices said, was a system of vast caverns. Artificially made caverns, inhabited by a race of people almost as ancient as the Earth itself, but a people mad and degenerate, a people left behind on a dying earth when the last rocket had left, eons before, for the stars. This race of people was not at all nice to know. They had a habit of feeding upon human flesh.

Shaver called them "dero."

Our religions and mythologies and legends of Atlantis and Lemuria, Shaver said, had some basis in fact. But these tales were based on facts dimmed and distorted by time, the faint memory of a race of giants that had come here from the blackness of space to seed the Earth with man.

But when the young Sun began to lose its outer shell of pure carbon and create its energies from the heavier elements that had originally condensed at its center, harmful radiation began to rain on the Earth. The Elder Race, equipped with great scientific knowledge and inventions, used rays to bore a vast network of caverns beneath the surface, where they would be protected from the radiation, could filter out the radioactive elements from the water they drank and the food they ate. The Titans and Atlanteans, as Shaver knew them through "thought records" preserved on metallic tapes, never aged. They knew the emanations from a radioactive sun were the cause of growing old. Even in the 1940's, Shaver pointed out, it was known that girls who decorated watch dials with radium paint, and had a habit of sticking the tips of their brushes into their mouths, died of a peculiar disease. They seemed to age quickly; girls of twenty soon appeared to be old women.

Knowing the Sun would become increasingly dangerous, the Elder Races decided it was time to migrate to another solar system heated by a young star. So they left.

Certain surface dwellers, left behind in the wild exodus the colonizers found even more urgent than anticipated, crept into the caves to sack the treasures left behind.

Included in the cosmic loot were huge stationary ray machines, created to diffuse helpful radiations upon those who used them, but left without proper directions. Without periodic changes of the filters which screened out and built up harmful charges, the machines eventually would twist and pervert the minds of those under exposure to the rays.

These degenerate people who once inhabited Earth's surface now live in the caves, and derive pleasure from terrorizing, torturing and exploiting surface people, actually contacting them to defraud them of money and possessions. Their rays, directed upon mankind, combined with the Sun's radiations, are responsible for men's folly, in, for example, warring against one another. The dero also playfully torture individuals, making them hear voices, and cause accidents on the surface of the earth and in the skies.

The dero engage in interplanetary traffic with evil beings from other planets. These contacts are responsible for the odd aerial phenomena people have been witnessing since the early 1940's.

The dero were the devils and witches of our folklores and religions; they, not spirits, communicate with mediums in trance, and materialize occasionally at seances through the use of rays.

Things could be worse in the caves, if it weren't for the good cavern people, whom Shaver termed "tero." Constantly they war on the evil dero, keeping them in check. In later days Shaver chose to move to Amherst, Wisconsin, because he said a large encampment of tero lived nearby, though he didn't enlarge on whether they lived on the surface or underground.

When Shaver's first story, "I Remember Lemuria," hit the newsstands in *Amazing Stories,* Palmer became less sure that Shaver was just imagining things, things which made extremely good reading and which an editor couldn't afford to pass up. Now, thousands of letters poured in from readers who said they didn't just *think* Shaver was right, they *knew* he was right. One letter was 34 pages long! Some of the correspondents, as Shaver believed he had done, said they actually had visited the caves. One writer claimed to have fought his way out of a cave in Burma, during World War II, with a submachine gun.

The circulation of *Amazing Stories* jumped to the incredible figure (for a science fiction "pulp" magazine) of 185,000.

The Shaver Mystery continued in the magazine for five years, without any signs of losing popularity. The number of confirmations that poured in from readers was a phenomenon that can now be compared, in public interest and apparent proofs, to the saucer mystery.

Suddenly *Amazing Stories* dropped the whole thing like a hot potato. From that point onward Palmer, until he resigned, printed only science fiction of the more orthodox type, the kind written as fiction, that held no claim to being true.

Life magazine said the Mystery was stopped by the hard core of organized science fiction fandom, outraged at seeing a pure form of literature adulterated by claims that it contained fact. The fans were sickened, the editors said, by the intrusion into science fiction fandom of what they termed the "lunatic fringe."

Others reported William B. Ziff, the publisher, didn't like the Mystery personally. Palmer, according to others who insisted they were in the know, had become fearful for his own safety after several remarkable visits to Shaver, at which times he heard some of Shaver's voices, threatening his life. It was hinted some unusual accidents had occurred, and Palmer himself admitted something that happened to his typewriter had given him a cold sweat.

Shaver said there was an ancient and almost unbreakable conspiracy to keep the secret of the caves, and those who pried into matters that did not concern them were in for trouble.

The question still remains, why did *Amazing Stories* drop a series that had made the publisher half a million dollars and was still going strong? Even if not a word of it were true, it is understood that pure philosophy butters precious little bread. Organized science fiction fandom was important, but its numbers were so small in comparison to the mass of non-organized general readers and those who swore by Shaver that the circulation of the magazine would not have been seriously impaired had organized fandom refused to purchase a single copy.

I didn't think then, nor do I now, that Shaver was perpetrating a hoax. Theory, detail and background may have come from his subconscious. But if that is so, Shaver has the most remarkable subconscious of any man living on this earth.

❂   ❂   ❂   ❂   ❂

After the Shaver episode, Palmer founded a magazine of his

own, *Fate,* one of the early vanguards of flying saucer reporting and investigation, for in those days "conventional" magazines wouldn't touch the subject, even with a ten-foot linotype.

Later Palmer created an even newer magazine, this one a straight science fiction publication called *Other Worlds,* and more recently another magazine not unlike *Fate,* titled *Mystic.*

Most science fiction magazines publish letters from readers. Readers seem to get a great charge out of writing long letters about each issue, often listing story by story and letting the editor know what they think about each one. Such readers are known as the hard core of science fiction fandom, the enthusiasts who often organize local fan clubs and even hold national conventions.

I had attended such a convention to find out what it was all about and afterward, still more confused than informed, often looked in occasional science fiction magazines I picked up from newsstands, for more information on what I thought was indeed an interesting movement.

If I were a psychologist I would probably write a book also about organized science fiction fandom. Professors would probably go about pondering it and some fan would probably slip into my home and shoot me. But, again if I were a psychologist it might be more interesting to psychoanalyze myself, to learn just why *I* like science fiction.

Anyway, it was through the letter columns of Palmer's magazine, *Other Worlds,* that I first found out about Bender.

A civilian investigating agency was being formed in Bridgeport, Conn., to look into the Flying Saucer Mystery, Albert K. Bender wrote. He called the organization The International Flying Saucer Bureau, welcomed membership and assistance.

I wrote to Bender, offering my help. I felt that a civilian

organization would be helpful, if only for informing members what was going on. Since the scope of government saucer investigation was not generally known at that time, I figured that civilian research might aid the nation in meeting any crisis the saucers might portend.

Bender replied enthusiastically to my letter of November 20, 1952, was particularly interested in hearing more about the West Virginia "monster" I told him of investigating. He would welcome my membership, but more important, he asked, would I become a representative of IFSB for the entire state. Representatives had already been appointed in fifteen states, and machinery was being set in motion to institute foreign chapters. The response to his letter in *Other Worlds* had been overwhelming.

V

Points North, South and West

"The mystery of the Flying Saucers," Bender had stated in an editorial in the first issue of the IFSB publication, *Space Review*, "will eventually be solved by calm, clear-thinking individuals."

This sounded to me like the thing I'd been looking for.

As West Virginia representative for the organization I solicited new memberships and reported saucer sightings occurring in my state. 1 also contributed articles to *Space Review*.

I was surprised to learn Bender was a young man, 31. For a

person of that age Bender had crammed a lot of experience into his short life.

He had served in the Air Force during World War II, had come to Bridgeport from West Pittston, Pennsylvania, after his discharge. In that short time he had worked himself up to an executive position in Acme Shear's Bridgeport plant.

When you sit down and talk to Bender you cannot help being impressed, and you are almost overwhelmed by his dominant personality. His piercing eyes seem to look right through you, yet his personality carries a warmth of good humor which makes a guest comfortable. Even though his conversation reflects a wide knowledge of almost anything you can bring up, Bender is careful to let you do your share of the talking.

One of the first things you realize is that in Bender, despite his absorption in a project that could engender wild thinking, logic always keeps a tight rein on imagination.

When you ask him about some of the dramatic claims made by some more unorthodox exponents of the saucer mystery, he does not baldly criticize them, but you can tell from his manner that he cannot be stampeded into crediting these somewhat wild tales.

"Maybe they're right. I really don't know. But I most certainly have some doubts."

I wondered how Bender could run such a large organization in his spare time, considering he was also an active member of the United States Rocket Society, which surely would command much attention.

A great many others contributed a lot of time to the IFSB, he explained. Members, particularly those who lived nearby in Bridgeport, pitched in with physical details of running the Bureau and were of inestimable help. Bender didn't mention that his ability as an executive enabled him to command the cooperation, respect, and hours of grueling, but thanks to his intelligent direction, fascinating work that went into running the organization.

Meanwhile *Space Review* was reporting a number of strange saucer events.

One account reminded me of the "monster" that had appeared in my own state. J. D. "Sonny" Desvergers of Palm Beach, Florida, came upon a hideous monster which shot at him with some kind of paralyzing ray. The terrifying event, which frightened Desvergers so profoundly that he staggered out of the woods babbling incoherently, occurred on August 19, 1952, less than a month before something out of the unknown held a reign of terror in the small West Virginia community of Flatwoods. Desvergers' encounter had also been signalized by a suffocating, nauseous odor.

Desvergers, a Scoutmaster, was driving three Boy Scouts home after a meeting. They swung onto Military Trail and were nearing Lantana when they saw a huge flying object, with windows like an airliner, apparently crash in a nearby palmetto thicket. Desvergers thought it odd that he didn't hear a crash, but as he reconstructed the events leading to his bizarre experience, he remembered he hadn't ascribed much importance to that fact. His paramount concern, at that point, was for the people who might be trapped in the "aircraft."

He grabbed a machete and leaped over the road bank.

"You boys stay here," he told his passengers. "These palmetto thickets are treacherous."

The Scoutmaster knew that if he wasn't careful he might step into quicksand.

"If I'm not back in ten minutes run up the road to that

house and call the sheriff," Desvergers instructed, referring to Deputy Sheriff Mott Partin, who subsequently investigated the area and swore he found a burned patch of ground where the Scoutmaster had his brush with the unknown, an encounter Desvergers says he could now explain if it weren't for security.

After cutting his way through about 200 yards of palmetto thicket Desvergers came to a clearing. Knowing such clearings well from near misses he had previously experienced in such terrain, he stepped gingerly, his eyes studying the ground. One careless step and he might be in quicksand. If the aircraft had crashed, he would run onto the wreckage any moment now. . . .

Then everything got hot, as if the Sun had suddenly come out. Only there was no light! The heat seemed to be coming from above. Desvergers looked up.

Where were the stars?

The Scoutmaster wondered, later, why there had been a delayed recognition that something was wrong—very wrong. He remembered thinking it was a clear night, that it must have become cloudy all of a sudden—while he wasted precious seconds.

Then he gathered the impression that something was overhead, blotting out the sky. In the next instant he had swung his lantern upward.

He was directly under the thing!

It was something made of metal, of a dirty-grayish color. It was so near he could have hit with his machete!

Terror struck the Scoutmaster. Terror so paralyzing he felt he couldn't move. He mumbled and tried to scream as he strove to force his muscles to work. Numb all over, he felt a tingling sensation throughout his body like one's foot when it is asleep.

His feet didn't seem to be touching the ground, but he knew they were, for finally he realized he was backing out, slowly dragging his feet backward while his head angled upward, his eyes fixed on the object.

"It was large enough for six or eight men to stand up in it," Desvergers told investigators. "I could see it was about ten feet high in the center as I kept my eyes fixed on it and finally backed from under it. The thing seemed to be moving away from me at the same time."

He then could see it from a right angle. He noticed it was shaped like "half a rubber ball," tapering down to about a three-foot thickness on the sides. Some kind of spectral glow shone around the contraption. The air was filled with a hissing noise.

His senses began creeping back. Why hadn't he heard the hissing noise when he was directly under it? Was that what made him look up? No, it was the terrifying heat, he remembered.

His returning faculties told him this was no ordinary aircraft, as he could now see the whole thing silhouetted against the sky. It appeared to be hovering about ten feet off the ground.

Suddenly something opened in the dome; Desvergers later guessed it was a porthole. That was almost the last thing he remembered until he came to his senses, stumbling near the road embankment, being supported by the sheriff and two of the Boy Scouts. He was mumbling, "I'm coming. . . . I'm coming. . . ."

When the porthole opened a ball of fire shot out at him. It seemed to float toward him, he remembered, misty, yet giving off sparks. There may have been heat connected with it, for whatever it was burned holes in his yachting cap, but it was the smell that overpowered all other sensations. The stench filled his throat and nostrils while he gasped for breath. Like the Flatwoods witnesses, he couldn't describe the odor.

"It was worse than rotten eggs, and something like burning flesh," he later told an investigator for *The Saucerian.* "Somehow I mean human flesh, though I've never smelled it burn. I suppose you think I'm all confused, and I suppose I am— I guess I meant to say I've really never smelled anything like it. It seemed to grip my throat and cut off my breath."

"Then I blacked out," Desvergers continued his narrative, "but right before that I saw the *thing.*"

"What kind of thing?" the investigator queried.

Some of the blood drained from Desvergers' face. He looked as if he were going to get sick.

"I—I can't tell you!"

"Do you mean it was too horrible to describe?"

"Let it go at that. I don't want to talk about it," and with that Desvergers tried to change the subject.

Thirty minutes passed before Deputy Partin arrived to find the Scoutmaster stumbling out of the thicket.

"If that boy wasn't scared he's a better actor than I'd give him credit for," the deputy declared. He also examined Desvergers, found the hair singed from his arm, which was reddened and looked as if it would blister.

Partin also saw the yachting cap. Later on Air Force investigators forwarded it to Wright Field, presumably to submit it to tests. They had lost no time in getting hold of Desvergers; he had been grilled for two hours behind closed doors at International Airport.

Whatever Desvergers had seen the Air Force didn't want publicized, beyond what he had already told the newspapers.

He was unable to answer many of the questions put to him. Most of these centered around the thing or creature he had seen.

It appeared strange that Desvergers could not find words to describe at least some detail connected with the creature he had viewed. He had put off some questioners by saying the thing was so horrible it disturbed him even to think about it, let alone describe it.

Since all this occurred when the flying saucer investigations I knew about were going ahead on an even keel, I took it for granted that the most important part of this incident was the fact that it added another eye-witness report to our record of saucer sightings. But when Bender abruptly went tight-lipped, and his actions became puzzling, I began thinking about some other statements Desvergers had made. Suddenly they gained new significance.

Air Force investigators had "opened the book" to Desvergers, to use his words, and had given him much of the information then officially known about saucers. "We don't have it here—it's not ours," the Scoutmaster told reporters, meaning the disks were not built by the United States government, though he refused to comment further on what the investigators had revealed to him.

Why had Air Force investigators briefed Desvergers on the salient facts then known about the saucer mystery, after hearing his story? There could be only one answer!

As a result of his encounter Desvergers had discovered a few things he must not be allowed to tell, a few key facts that might crack saucers wide open for a lot of people and lead them to demand more facts. By acquainting Desvergers with current Air Force knowledge of the disks they could accomplish a double purpose: first of all they might convince Desvergers it would be harmful to publicize that part of his experience, and secondly before imparting the knowledge they would have an excuse to place him under security regulations!

"I know what it is and it's of vital importance," said Desvergers, "but it's better for me not to go any farther for the public good because it may cause another Orson Welles panic."

Later I remembered he sounded a lot like Bender.

About a year after the occurrence the Air Force adopted a standard explanation to discredit the Desvergers story. Go to the Pentagon and ask what they think of Desvergers and you'll see a regulation performance repeated for your benefit. First a little smile will form on the officer's face. Then he'll tell you that they've been investigating and find that at one point in Desvergers' Marine Corps career during World War II a "certain thing" happened. They won't say just what it was, but with raised eyebrows they will hint it was something quite damaging to the Floridan's reputation.

In the course of many men's service careers they commit indiscretions of one sort or another, which are seldom held against them in civilian life. Although a suggestible person may begin by discrediting Desvergers' story because of "a certain thing" that happened in his service career, upon thought the idea becomes ridiculous. The investigator cannot help wondering how far officialdom will go to cover up the truth about flying saucers.

Perhaps Desvergers was never under security after his untoward experience. Perhaps he was prevented from relating key parts of his story through fear of some kind of official and legal blackmail!

Space Review also reported that Frank Edwards, Mutual Broadcasting System newscaster, had interviewed Bill Squyres, a radio entertainer of Station KOAM, Pittsburg, Kansas, who had a close brush with a saucer on his way to an early morning broadcast on August 24, 1952.

For a saucer, it must have been an old model. For Squyres swore it had propellers all around the middle. But it was like nothing ever before seen on Earth.

Squyres lives at Frontenac, Kansas, about nine miles from the station. On his way to work, about six A.M. he received the shock of his life.

"My hair rose straight up the back of my head," he commented, when relating the strange experience.

He was driving through a heavily wooded area seven and a half miles from Pittsburg when he ran across the weird contraption, hovering about ten feet from the ground. He jammed on the brakes, pulled over onto the shoulder of the road, and just sat there looking at it, unable to believe what he was seeing.

"It looked like two turtle shells or two platters joined together," had a dull, aluminum appearance. "It was about 75 feet long and about two-thirds as wide." At one end of it, which he presumed was the front, he saw what apparently was a control cabin, with the figure of a human-like creature sitting there, though he could see the figure only from the shoulders up. At first Squyres thought the thing was an ordinary airplane, but then he saw the intense blue light. In the middle of the strange craft were more windows, also lighted by the eerie blue light, which pulsated from dark to light blue. Squyre's eyes then glued themselves to the windows of the thing, for he could now see people or something *moving*, as if in great agitation. The side windows must have been translucent, however, for Squyres said he could discern only shadows, such as one would see on a window shade pulled down in front of moving people in a lighted room at night.

A throbbing sound came from the machine, which he said was "sort of wiggling" or oscillating.

Marshalling courage, Squyres decided to have a closer look, and got out of his car. When he slammed the car door the thing took off, straight upward "like a light cord when you release it."

"It sounded like a covey of a hundred quail taking off," he said, trying to describe the humming noise as it accelerated.

He jumped into the car and drove hurriedly to the station, visibly trembling as he related the story to the early morning staff. George Massey, an announcer; Leo Stafford, chief engineer; Marcel Stewart, salesman, and Squyres all drove back to the location. The saucer had left little evidence, only some weeds which had been blown down, apparently, thought Squyres, by the backwash of the propellers.

Residents of Pittsburg were incredulous, though they had no reason to doubt the entertainer, who had a reputation for veracity. Squyres was married, 42 years old and the father of two children. He was considered by those who knew him to be a responsible citizen.

The witness never did state whether Air Force investigators had interrogated him, but one cryptic remark he made remains in the files of the *Neosho Daily Democrat,* which investigated the incident.

"They're not about to make me retract this information," Squyres had stated. "I'm not going to let them give me shots or anything else to make me say I didn't see it!"

This famous Pittsburg sighting is obviously Case No. 12 in the "12 good sightings" listed in the 316-page *Project Blue*

Book Special Report No. 14, deliberately slanted, according to some investigators, to minimize in the public mind the possibility that saucers come from space. No names or places are given in the *Report,* but the details are obviously similar.

The account reminded me of another report I had just received, one of many recorded in that saucer-ridden summer of 1952, when many incredulous citizens found themselves within a few feet of something unknown and alien.

The main feature of the comparison that struck me was that Mrs. Flora Rogers described the thing she saw as "shaped just like a turtle."

Although not prodigious for a Texas saucer, the flying machine that Mrs. Rogers, a Martin County ranch woman, could have almost touched, was certainly, in her opinion, quite out of this world.

The thing must have been preparing to land when its pilot saw her, the ranch woman declared, since it descended toward her slowly, about ten to fifteen miles per hour, she estimated, and passed close to her before zooming up into the sky. Because it was only about 20 feet in the air and passed just across the pasture road from her, Mrs. Rogers was able to relate what perhaps is the best description of a saucer ever recorded.

When she first noticed its movements, stopped her car and leaned out the window, she assumed it was an airplane coming in for a forced landing. Soon she knew she must be mistaken. This was like no airplane on Earth!

It was coming down from a westerly direction, seemed to be "wobbling in mid-air" as it slowly came toward her and the ground.

Not yet quite registering the alien appearance of the craft, Mrs. Rogers observed it calmly, not foreseeing the terror that would soon strike her. She could see the object was shaped like a turtle or rather, as was the Pittsburg saucer, like two turtle shells joined by a rim, although the top "shell" on this one overhung the lower "shell" by three or four inches.

A crack or slit circled the odd flying machine, and from the slit three paddle-like things protruded. The paddles, which resembled boat oars, "moved slowly back and forth in a smooth motion," and she could see plainly where they were fastened to the machine.

The object was, she estimated, ten feet long by about fifteen feet wide, determining the orientation of length and width by the direction in which it was flying. The bulging middle, however, seemed to be only about three feet thick.

Asked if she thought there was room for a man to pilot the machine, Mrs. Rogers said she believed there was room, stating, however, that she saw no windows nor doors in it, nor any sign of occupants.

No lights of any kind were visible, even in the crack around the machine.

"There was, however," she added, "a spout sticking out of the back resembling a tail-pipe. A blue flame, similar to a butane flame, was coming from this spout. There was no sound at all from the machine."

She remembered the saucer was camouflaged both on the top and bottom with a "sort of greenish-gray and brown shade." It resembled the olive drab used by the Army for camouflage during the last war, she told reporters of the *Big Spring Weekly News*.

After the machine flew past her it suddenly began an ascent at a speed almost too fast for the eye to see, as she described it, adding it was out of sight "in seconds." Mrs. Rogers estimated she had watched it at least four minutes before it departed.

Not until she witnessed the tremendous speed at which it zoomed into the sky did she become frightened. Suddenly she realized she had witnessed something unearthly.

She leaned against the car, now trembling, and so shaken she had to exert great effort to raise her feet into the car.

"I drove the eighteen miles to Garden City, most of which was dirt road, in 25 minutes, not stopping for a light or anything, I was so scared," she told the sheriff upon her arrival.

The sheriff believed Mrs. Rogers and sent out a search party. It was reported that the Goodfellow Air Force Base of San Angelo later sent planes to search for the object. The investigation drew a blank.

But nothing could shake Mrs. Rogers' story or her belief in what she had seen.

"I have lived a long time and what I saw was certainly no mirage," she said. "What it was I don't know," she added, "but I know I saw it."

Mrs. Rogers related her story with such straightforwardness that neighbors could not help believing she was telling the truth, though few could venture an opinion as to what she saw.

When pressed for an opinion as to what she thought the object represented, Mrs. Rogers hazarded a guess, but insisted it was only an idea she had evolved while watching it.

"It must have been some sort of radar machine taking pictures of the ground beneath."

And so ended another flying saucer story few people would believe, except those who heard her tell it first hand, a story that would be discounted by the Air Force and forgotten by all but the few who had the temerity to collect and file away data on such unusual and unlikely events.

Space Review continued with another close-range sighting. A farmer in Conway, South Carolina, had taken a pot shot at a saucer hovering over his barn. Hearing the livestock in a turmoil he grabbed his gun, went outside the house to investigate. There at treetop level was a strange contraption about 24 feet across and about 12 feet wide, of light grayish color. "It was something like half an egg, cut from end to end," he told investigators, adding he had shot at it, heard the bullet ricochet. When the bullet struck it the saucer, or whatever it was, flew away. *Space Review* reported numerous livestock had died in the area after the occurrence.

Meanwhile, in Stuttgart Germany, 200 scientists from twelve countries, meeting in the third International Astronautical Congress, stated saucers were not from Mars or any other planet. They said they were merely optical and atmospheric illusions, *Space Review* reported.

❀　❀　❀　❀　❀

The eye-witness accounts piled up in our files. We analyzed them and assessed them and compared them, looking for corroborative details and sometimes succeeding, looking for contradictions, looking for hoaxes, looking for a key that would unlock the mystery. More and more new members joined the IFSB. In the course of my work for the Bureau I met some of its other active representatives. One of these men was Dominick C. Lucchesi of Jersey City.

Dominick C. Lucchesi is, underneath it all, a materialist. He doesn't believe entirely in the occult, nor Shaver, nor interplanetary saucers. But he would like unsuspecting friends to think he does. With him such matters are hobbies and intellectual exercises. During working hours he is a highly-paid gyroscope technician; off duty he amuses friends by telling them how he has projected his astral body. I wondered where he picked up all the terms and shop-talk of occultism. When I went to his house I found out. He is a collector of unusual books, and his wife continually goes on, half-way in fun, about how her projected fur coats and new Cadillacs end up on the book shelf.

He got into flying saucers through Bender. Once he told me he wished to make a materialistic approach to saucers, and claimed he could actually build a terrestrial flying saucer if he had the facilities. He hinted that Earth-made saucers might already be in the skies.

Another of these men was August C. Roberts, who, as did Lucchesi, became a close friend of mine through our work for the Bureau.

By profession "Augie," as his friends call him, is a free lance photographer. He has not always been interested in saucers; the public was aware of their existence and curious about their origins long before his eyes and ears were opened to the subject. In those long-past days he spent his spare time engaging in "normal" activities, such as archery and skin diving.

All that was changed, on a Ground Observer Corps skywatch tower that night of July 27, 1952.

It seem that many people must personally see a saucer before they are convinced something unusual is troubling the heavens. It may have been like that with Augie.

George Conger, James Leyden and Roberts were on duty in the tower surveying the skies, not expecting to see what suddenly flashed across the skyline.

"Hey, Roberts, lend me those glasses a minute," Conger shouted. "I've been watching a light there in the East by the Empire State Building and it's acting funny. It's no plane, I can tell that!"

He looked through the glasses.

"Jimmy, come out here and take a look at that damn light," he called to Leyden.

"What the devil is it?" Leyden muttered incredulously.

To Roberts it was clearly circular in shape, slightly smaller than a ten cent piece held at arm's length. Through the binoculars it appeared to be as large as a half-dollar. It was definitely disk-shaped, as it presented part of its rim toward the observers. Roberts said that through the binoculars the thickness of the disk appeared to be that of two half-dollars put together. Judging the size by comparing it with that of planes often seen in that particular area, Roberts estimated the object to be anywhere from 50 to 100 feet in diameter.

"When I first saw the disk," Roberts told newsmen, "the rim was a brownish color. The inner part of the disk was a bright orange, with a brownish dot in the exact center. The entire object was glowing and flickering. Through the binoculars I could clearly see the rim spinning in a clockwise direction. As the entire object moved the outer rim changed to a reddish brown, and the dot in the center changed color along with the rim. I noticed the object flickered less while the rim was spinning. When the thing finally departed, the colors changed again: the rim and dot in the center became a glowing red, and the orange color in the center became a paler orange. As it left I could again clearly discern the edge of the disk."

Roberts, not thinking about flying saucers, nor greatly interested in them for that matter, did not have a camera with him, but grabbed one Conger had with him and made two exposures.

It was an old camera and the shutter stuck on slow speeds. As a result Roberts got a time exposure of the object, complicated by the movement of the camera, but there was enough detail on one of the negatives to prove what they saw was real.

While the spectacular sighting was in progress Roberts got an Air Force official on the phone through the local filter center, described the actions and appearance of the disk in detail. The official told Roberts the visual sighting had been confirmed by radar.

In watching the thing over the New York skyline Roberts knew there was something wondrous about it. The experience made him realize beyond all shadow of a doubt here was a machine of some kind, intelligently controlled, but a machine entirely out of this world, outstripping mankind's puny science.

In talking with hundreds who have seen what they swear were saucers I have run into an attitude about the mystery that is, though hard to explain, perhaps indicative of an important key to a solution. These viewings have affected people in some emotional manner. Maybe it is because of the sensation that they have seen something alien and unknown, something perhaps from space. Usually such persons immediately begin to read and investigate, to try to find some explanation for what they have witnessed. Maybe it is a subconscious drive to preserve reason.

After he photographed the saucer Roberts received widespread publicity. His was one of the first photographs to be authenticated by witnesses.

Maybe the publicity helped to arouse Roberts' interest, but I believe one important factor is contained in a set of photographs taken at a different time, three years before he consciously pointed his camera at the sky to photograph an unknown object.

When he had developed the set of photographs he ascribed nothing unusual to them. But three years later, when he examined them by chance, he found some objects on them, objects that by all the rules of photography should not be there!

Roberts lives on the Jersey Shore. The New York City skyline stretches before him in behemoth panorama. But it is something he sees constantly, a sight dulled by familiarity. He stopped photographing it years ago.

The bewildering photographs were made on a night when he had a particular reason for photographing the skyline. The Air Force had announced a special test over New York City, and Hoboken, New Jersey, in June, 1949. They would drop flash bombs to test the effectiveness of illuminating a city for photographing it after dark. The test received wide advance publicity so that residents would not be alarmed by the flares.

Roberts decided to try his own luck at some shots, and made a number of exposures while the flares were being dropped.

Since he knew the papers would be full of pictures of the tests the next morning, he developed the negatives, noted they had come out satisfactorily, and put them aside, not bothering to make prints from them.

Although he did note some ball-like objects on the negatives, Roberts took little notice of them. At that time he had never given any thought to flying saucers. Not until later did he remember that while he was making the photographs a friend had shouted, "What was that!" Since then the friend had moved away and Roberts did not know where to reach him.

Roberts rediscovered the objects when Bender asked him to

write an article for *Space Review,* instructing members how to take pictures of unidentified objects at night. To check his data, Roberts dug one of the flash bomb negatives from his files. There were the objects he had noticed before, without ascribing importance to them. He started. What were they?

With trembling fingers he agitated the developing solution and saw the things slowly take form under the amber dark-room lamp.

Surely they represented some sort of lens flare phenomena, common in photography, results of the glare from the flash bombs.

He printed the other negatives, feeling sure they held no great importance. One negative, however, puzzled him. No flash bombs were in this picture, a time exposure of the skyline with a street lamp in the foreground. One of the things appeared in this picture also! It was round and conelike, apparently was a three-dimensional object! It appeared to be in the sky somewhere above the street lamp, not at great altitude, for the source for illuminating the object obviously was the street lamp itself!

Shadow covered part of the thing, as if the conelike shape (its tip facing the camera) caught part of the light and prevented its falling over the rest of the object.

Roberts' native conservatism shouted it surely was the result of a lens flare, but he took it to another professional photographer for consultation. The other man examined the prints closely. Although he believed that the pictures taken of the flares could possibly contain flash-back from the lens, he admitted that the shot that included the street lamp had him stumped.

Roberts had seen nothing when he took the pictures. That may be why he advances no claims for them and deliberately asserts, to some people, that the "saucers" are only reflections. But since 1949 Roberts has learned that other "things," invisible to the eye, have turned up on film, things that could not possibly be tricks of camera lenses. Meanwhile experts who examine his flash bomb photographs continue to be baffled.

✿   ✿   ✿   ✿   ✿

I don't know the exact date, but it was sometime near the end of January, 1953 when I received a telephone call from Bender. I had never talked with him personally before; contacts had been by mail.

Bender's manner of talking impressed me. He sounded like a man who was very serious about saucers. His voice reverberated with a boundless enthusiasm and aggressiveness. I remember thinking that if anyone could lead a group of investigators in pulling back the veil of saucer secrecy it would be a man like Bender.

"I want to ask you a favor," he said, after several personal amenities. "Don't say yes if you can't handle it, or for friendship's sake. It's going to be a big job, and it's going to take up a lot of your time."

"Let's have it, Al," I replied, confessing excitement, I am sure, in the tone of my voice.

"This thing is getting too big for us in Bridgeport. I have some fine people helping me, but there's a limit to what they can do. We're bogged down in paper work. It seems we can't get out from under it, Gray. Someone casually seeing our letterheads probably would think we're a bunch of big shots who do nothing but chase saucers. They'd never realize we're just people who have regular jobs and businesses and have to do this sort of thing on the side, in our spare time."

"If there's anything I can do to help, you know I'll try, Al."

"Mars has been close this year. I'm not saying that's where

they're coming from, though Lonzo Dove thinks they may be using Mars as a way station. Dove has been working on the Mars theory for some time. The guy's an astronomer, you know. Seems to be a level-headed fellow, not one of those crackpots."

Yes, I had heard of Dove, I told Al. I had read some of his material in *Space Review*.

"There's a lot of it we haven't printed. Don't get me wrong, it isn't classified. Not anything like that, at least as far as I know. Anyway, Dove reached his conclusions independently. He has been examining our files, and on the surface I'd have to agree it *does* look like Mars. Now you're no astronomer, Gray, but I think you know something of how the planets orbit around the Earth."

Mars, reviewed Bender, swings close to Earth about every two years, such proximity being termed opposition. During the present series of oppositions these swings were becoming more and more what astronomers termed "favorable."

"By 'favorable' I mean that every two years through 1956, Mars will be increasingly closer to Earth. In 1954 Mars will come within 40,300,000 miles, and in 1956, it will be the closest since 1924."

Dove had made a careful check on sightings, found they definitely increased in numbers during periods of favorable opposition.

Sightings were still poring in from the summer and fall of 1952, when Mars had been near.

"Some people are just now hearing about us and are sending in details on what they saw. Some of it is astounding! We'd like to investigate some of these sightings very carefully, though we can't possibly cope with all of them. Here's where you come in if you can handle it."

Bender said he was setting up a Department of Investigation within the Bureau, was assigning it the job of running down selected sightings in fuller detail. He was appointing some experts in the field of aeronautics, photography and astronomy to analyze sightings.

"If I sound juvenile, don't get me wrong. It's no exciting cloak and dagger thing. It's mainly a lot of hard work. And remember, we're probably the most bankrupt group of 'experts' in America today, so there won't be any expense accounts or salaries. But I think our accomplishments will more than repay us for our trouble."

"But I'm no expert," I remonstrated, mentioning that I knew a little about almost everything and not much in particular about any scientific field.

'I have the experts. What we need is leadership and someone with the executive ability to keep prodding them and to organize what they have found out. You're the man, Gray."

I thanked him for the compliment, but said he'd probably received an overdone impression of my abilities from somewhere.

"I want you to accept the post of Chief Investigator."

This floored me.

"In accepting this position, I hope you'll keep in mind something I said previously. This is no cloak and dagger project, though I'll admit 'Chief Investigator' does sound dramatic. It's mainly just plain old hard work."

I paused on the phone. My own work with *The Saucerian* was taking too much of my time. But Bender's project sounded important, and urgent.

"I'll telegraph you my decision tomorrow, Al," I told him, "but I think I can tell you now that telegram is going to say 'yes.' "

It did.

Bender appointed Lucchesi to the post of aeronautical consultant. Many sightings involved aircraft of new configuration, and perhaps in the back of Bender's mind was the thought that the Air Force might have something that compared to a saucer up there, but a machine which worked on conventional terrestrial mechanical principles. Dove would take care of astronomical research. Rev. S. L. Daw, a Washington, D.C., clergyman, would assist in general investigation. He had experience in police methods of investigation through work in rehabilitation of juvenile delinquents, but what was more important, Bender explained, Rev. Daw would be helpful when witnesses might ascribe a religious connotation to sightings.

"If the secret of flying saucers develops to include an extraterrestrial origin, I'm afraid it's going to have a great effect on religion," Bender once told me. By the way he talked, he was worried.

The other member of the Department was Augie Roberts, who was to act as consultant on any case involving photographs.

Roberts made a good many investigations for the Department. Some of them were productive, some were not. None had far-reaching results—with the possible exception of the trip he took to New Haven, Connecticut, to track down an amazing fireball seen in that city.

August 20, 1953, was the day the world was supposed to come to an end, according to certain prophets who evolved that startling prediction after poking around in the damp darkness inside the Great Pyramid of Egypt.

That particular prediction of world doom wasn't publicized widely. Perhaps its prognosticators were occultists who comfortably did not believe even their own prophecies. But if any pyramidologists, as members of this school of prophets are termed, were operating in New Haven on that date, they likely had quite a scare.

For at about nine P.M. on that date residents heard a great swoosh. Buildings trembled and lights dimmed. Some cried an A-bomb had fallen. One woman had a miscarriage as a result of the excitement.

Only one resident, a motorist, saw the object responsible for the panic. A red ball of fire about six to eight inches in diameter smashed through a signboard, changed its course, tore through the top of a large tree, just missing telephone and power lines, and disappeared over a hill about a half-mile away.

The fire department rushed to investigate the smoking, half-demolished sign. They couldn't explain what ripped the hole, more than a foot wide, through 20-gauge steel. Whatever hit the signboard had struck with terrific impact.

Nearby Naval Ordnance investigators also rushed to the scene, but would make no comment.

Roberts found that whatever had struck the signboard left behind a calling card. He pried loose a sample of some kind of metal, unlike that which formed the signboard and obviously not a part of it. He sent a section to Bender for analysis.

Bender never did announce a result of the analysis, made, according to one saucer investigator, at Oak Ridge, Tennessee. Maybe he had a good reason, I thought later, after I learned what had happened in Bridgeport.

Later Bender said the analysis had nothing to do with the matter, but by that time there were a lot of things Bender couldn't talk about.

The thing that happened to him was to happen to other investigators—after they had in their possessions certain pieces of metal, deposits that must have been actual parts of or residue from UFO's.

Whatever happened brought Bender's investigation of flying saucers to a startling climax—and a terrifying end.

When some other investigators got wind of the incident, but not all of the facts, they laughed. Bender dreamed it all up, they declared.

But Bender wasn't laughing.

He was too frightened.

❈ ❈ ❈ ❈ ❈

Three men in black suits with threatening expressions on their faces. Three men who walk in on you and make certain demands.

Three men who know that *you* know what the saucers really are!

They don't want you to tell anyone else what you know.

The answer had hit you like a flash, one night when you had gone to bed after running all the theories through the hopper of your brain. You had sat up in bed, snapped your fingers, and said, "This is IT! I KNOW I have the ANSWER!

The next day the theory didn't sound as convincing to you as it did the night before. Nevertheless it was a good one, and you had certain data which would more than half-way prove it. You wrote this down and sent it to someone. When the three men came into your house one of them had that very same piece of paper in his hand.

They said that you, among the thousands working on the same thing, had hit pay dirt. *You* had the *answer!* Then they filled you in with the details.

After they got through with you, you wished you'd have never heard of the word, "saucer."

You turned pale and got awfully sick.

You couldn't get anything to stay on your stomach for three long days.

VI

Jersey City, New Jersey

I do not wish to get Bender into trouble. I don't believe publishing this information will endanger him. If I did, I'd keep my mouth shut.

I believe Bender handled himself too well for trouble. Some of the information he gave us may have been intended to lead us away from an actual solution. If that was the case I can heartily appreciate his position.

If Bender was closed down by the United States government, the three men probably had good reasons. But Bender never told us who the three men were, or who sent them, only that they "showed credentials." But government men do not dress so conspicuously, especially if they are on a secret mission. All the three men were dressed similarly—in black.

I am not certain they were government men who frightened Bender almost out of reason that unusual day in September, 1953, though I believe Bender steered our conjectures in that direction.

Much evidence does seem to point to government intervention, and to fit together, at least chronologically. For example, there was the matter of the business card, the FBI, and a confidential report Lucchesi either lost or had stolen from him.

But let us speak of the matters in order of occurrence.

We first come to the business card.

Bender probably is adept at amateur psychology. He sent me a quantity of business cards which presented me as Chief Investigator for the IFSB. He probably knew the cards would swell my ego and provide a conversation piece among my Clarksburg friends and business acquaintances who still thought saucers were the bunk.

I did give out four or five of them to close friends, who still had them when I checked with them one week later.

I have always been puzzled about just how the Federal Bureau of Investigation got hold of one of them.

For the local FBI agent walked into my office on August 28, 1953, flashed his credentials and also one of my business cards.

"What's this all about?" he asked me.

FBI agents usually do not scare me, but I was greatly taken aback by the visit. How had he obtained the card so soon after it had been printed? Was my saucer research contrary to the law in any fashion?

95

I nervously pulled out some of the files on the IFSB, explained it was an organization formed to investigate flying saucer phenomena, and that the Department of Investigation was merely a means of checking certain reports. I showed him a letter I had just received from headquarters, pointing to the investigating staff and other information on the letterhead. He gave the letterhead a careless, superficial glance, and handed it back to me.

Then he asked if I knew a certain individual, whose name, in my puzzlement, I failed to write down and which I subsequently forgot.

I told him I did not know the man.

He had written the name, and a Florida address, on the back of the business card. He explained the individual was apparently the victim of epilepsy, had been picked up downtown and was in St. Mary's Hospital. The card had been found among the patient's belongings and he was just checking to see if I knew him.

He thanked me, said that was all he wanted to know. I might add that all of this was conducted with deadpan expressions with no show of humor in connection with saucers.

He walked out of the office.

Then it struck me.

How in the world had anyone from Florida come into possession of one of my business cards?

It was the height of illogic.

I picked up the phone and called Bridgeport. Al was away on vacation, his stepfather informed the long distance operator.

I racked my mind. Had I given a card to any stranger? Come to think of it, I *had.* But the recipient had been a service man to whom I had given a lift while driving south to my country home, about 75 miles south of Clarksburg. The man said he was going to Charleston, West Virginia. Somehow (as it usually does when I talk with someone) the subject of saucers came up, and I gave him one of the cards when I let him out near Sutton at the point where I turned off onto a secondary road.

I couldn't see any connection between the service man and an epileptic from Florida.

I wondered if there was really an epileptic.

I thought of checking with the hospital, but after thinking it over I wondered if all were going well with our organization, and if we might be in some sort of trouble, or might be investigating something the government would rather we kept our hands off.

I sent a special report of the visit to Bender:

"In my opinion the interrogation was quite routine and perhaps only to learn more about the man in the hospital. I should think, however, that the information on the business card and whatever I told them will go into whatever kind of report they prepare on cases.

"The FBI is probably unconcerned about the flying saucer mystery, although one cannot be sure.

"In the event the FBI *is* concerned with the mystery, it would seem quite logical that IFSB members and officers might be interrogated further. It would seem to me the FBI might be curious as to what we're up to and check just to make sure we're O.K.

"If the government should become alarmed about flying saucers (assuming they are not already) IFSB members and officers might be questioned, and material in their files 'requested.'

"It might be wise to obtain legal opinion in view of preparing a directive to those in the Bureau who are in possession of our official reports and documented evidence of flying saucers. This directive would explain the rights of the individual against seizure of photographs and other materials, and comment upon what duties of a citizen would require giving out otherwise confidential information.

"This is not to suggest that the government is alarmed about flying saucers, that they might discourage civilian investigation of the mystery, or that they are seizing materials.

"It is my opinion that in the event of a big saucer scare such might come about.

"I think a clear outline of policy should be laid down which would take care of any situation that might develop."

Apparently Bender returned from his vacation about the ninth of September, for that was the date on which he replied to my special report.

He wrote that he was greatly surprised to find the FBI was investigating us. "I cannot for the life of me see why they would be checking up. It certainly proves one thing—the government is more interested in the saucers than we realize. It may bring about a big story for IFSB."

One member, who lived in Florida, was called to my attention. He had changed his address four times. First he lived in Norfolk, Virginia, then at three different places in Florida. While living in Virginia he had been a state representative for IFSB, but had resigned, stating he would be working for the government and all data he collected would be confidential. He was still a member, however, and still received *Space Review*.

On the same day Bender wrote to me, however, he called a meeting of the IFSB local staff in Bridgeport, according to the October, 1953, issue of *Space Review*.

They agreed upon a statement to be published in that issue:

"After serious consideration of all aspects involved in the operation of the International Flying Saucer Bureau, it has been decided to completely reorganize. Effective January 1, 1954, we will no longer be known as the International Flying Saucer Bureau, which specialized only in the mystery of the Flying Saucer."

Even then it would appear Bender was holding back something from me. Something that later on he would describe only to a few close friends.

In his September 9 letter Bender also noted it was careless of Lucchesi to have let an IFSB report slip out of his possession.

Which brings us to another mystery, which may or may not have had some connection with the odd goings-on at Bridgeport.

The Curilovic Case was routine. Nevertheless the Department of Investigation followed it through in the same careful procedure they followed with more dramatic sightings.

Mark R. Curilovic had submitted a photograph containing a saucer-like image. It pictured a sunset over Lake Erie, which Curilovic had shot without seeing any unusual object in the view-finder. The things in the picture were obviously lens reflections, Roberts immediately concluded upon examining the negative and print.

Nevertheless the Department decided the full investigative procedure should be afforded the case, and the careful procedure of its membership can be noted in the following quote from what we officially termed the Curilovic Saucer Report:

Procedure of Investigation: Original Curilovic Report, dated June 8, 1953, was mailed to Barker on that date by Headquarters, with instructions to process it through the Department, and to reach a decision on authenticity of the Report and photographs. A copy of these instructions, along with a letter Barker dispatched to Curilovic, was sent to Dove, Roberts, Lucchesi and Daw on June 8, 1953. The original photographic print was sent to Roberts, with instructions to investigate and forward to other members. Barker wrote Curilovic, and was able to secure negatives, and further information. Negatives were forwarded to Roberts, who printed copies in 8 x 10 size in sufficient quantity to be circulated immediately among the members. A digest of Roberts' opinion was attached.

Staff members then submitted their various opinions as to the authenticity of the report.

Barker sent a letter to Curilovic on August 12, advising him of the Department's decision, and returning prints and negatives he had sent.

The Curilovic Report concluded with the following *Verdict:*

After weighing the opinions of the Staff, it is apparent that the saucer-like image in the photograph is not an object defined by the Bureau as a Flying Saucer, but was caused by lens reflections in the camera used. This opinion is strengthened by the fact that Curilovic did not see any abnormal phenomena, nor did the other witnesses, when the photographs were taken.

All other data and observations appear to be reliable and the reporter honest.

It is therefore the verdict of the Department that until such time that new evidence might appear to change the opinion of the Staff, the photographs are not considered authentic in respect to containing images of Flying Saucers. Mark R. Curilovic, however, is commended for the clear and honest manner in which he submitted the information to the Bureau.

The report then listed various enclosures going with the master copy and filed at IFSB headquarters in Bridgeport.

Would-be researchers, fired by the enthusiasm of a sighting, or after hearing a few lurid accounts, often rush into the saucer mystery roughshod, expecting to dispose of the entire enigma in a week or a month.

After they discover the volume of work involved in checking on an endless progression of tiring, undramatic, or even deliberately faked data, their enthusiasm is often short-lived. The Curilovic Case is an example of the blanks so often drawn after enthusiastic investigators feel they have something that might be meaningful, just might be that final link in the giant jigsaw of saucerdom.

Members of the Department were level-headed and patient enough to realize, fortunately, that a weeding-out was often as important as an adding-to. For surely there was a nucleus of real phenomena, concrete and discoverable. But it might be a small nucleus. Once that nucleus was pinned down the jigsaw might fall into place.

I am not deliberately boring you with administrative details of an investigation department that is now defunct, though not by our own choosing.

If the Curilovic Report was intrinsically dull, it figured in a situation much more intriguing.

It in itself may some day turn out to have been a key, not for what it contained, but for *who* was concerned with it.

This was the report Lucchesi lost late in August, 1953.

101

Roberts was cursing over a new electric typewriter he was learning to use, apologizing for the appearance of the report he was writing for me.

To complicate matters the telephone kept ringing, with this and that friend on the line.

Roberts included an account of one of these calls in the letter he was writing me.

It was from the Hudson County Police.

There were three police forces in Jersey City, Roberts explained lengthily, while I skipped down through the letter to find out what was on the mind of the law, regarding, I suspected, the usual subject with Roberts—saucers. But Roberts is taxing when it comes to details. There was the City Police, the Hudson County Boulevard Police, and the other force simply called the Hudson County Police.

He had to explain what each of them did and where each was located.

Then he got to Lieutenant Kellegher.

Kellegher told Roberts a policeman had found a report that seemingly belonged to him, because his name was on it. He read off the other names, including my own, added it was about flying saucers.

Roberts knew immediately that it was the Curilovic Report.

"Come on over and pick it up. It's about lunch time, but I'll wait up on you," Lieutenant Kellegher promised, then gave directions for finding the police station.

Roberts glanced at his desk top. The Curilovic Report was lying there. Lucchesi must have lost his, for he was the only other person in Jersey City who would have one.

He tried to telephone Lucchesi, but the line was busy.

That was 11:30. He jumped into the car and drove to the

Hudson County Police station to which he had been directed. He arrived there at 11:52 (he had ascribed enough importance to the call to look at his watch). Somehow to him it seemed that not all was exactly right.

It wasn't.

He asked the desk sergeant for Lieutenant Kellegher.

The lieutenant wasn't there, the sergeant told him.

Roberts insisted he must be there, for he had promised to wait for him.

"Kellegher must have left your property in the record room," he was told. "Go down there and ask for King."

King turned out to be a detective, but a detective who knew nothing whatsoever about a lost report. When Roberts insisted that Kellegher had phoned him, and that he must have had the report in his possession because he was reading from it, King said, "Look, I'll show you in the books."

He opened a book, evidently a volume for writing down things that had been found. There was no listing of a lost flying saucer report.

King suggested he return the next morning.

By this time Roberts was becoming even more suspicious. He stopped at Lucchesi's house, gave him a quick rundown on the situation.

"You know I don't lose things," Dom insisted. "Look, it's right in here."

He opened the desk drawer, thumbed through the mail.

"I'll be damned! I was sure it was here—with the bills!"

Where could he have lost it?

I continue to become involved with interesting people. But we must not digress too far with Dom's brother, Armand. A book could be written about the fellow.

If Armand were a genius, he surely would be classified as a mad one. But I think it's all put on.

Maybe it's because I know little of electronics and because "Om," as he is nicknamed, gets a kick out of pulling my leg.

Om's basement is filled with banks of glowing vacuum tubes and weird-looking electronic devices he has constructed. It looks something like a mad doctor's laboratory. I have never seen a mad doctor's laboratory, except in the movies or on TV, and I suspect that in reality genuine mad doctors exert an effort to make their laboratories look more respectable. Otherwise they would be discovered for what they are. And I suspect that these perhaps thousands of mad doctors, cloaked in their show of respectability, do not want publicity.

I need not say that Om's basement showmanship is only a hobby. At his job he is a fine and serious engineer.

To visit Om's basement is at once dramatic and hilarious. He is engaged in cooking up Secret Inventions, and his electronic double-talk is convincing to someone unfamiliar with that field. He can give you actual directions for building a simple, inexpensive hydrogen bomb in your own home, a bomb I am suspiciously afraid just might work if someone were brave enough to put it together. But, as Om assured me, it lacks the capacity to blow up more than one or two city blocks.

What impressed me most in Om's "laboratory" was a device which he claimed would take electrical power right out of the air, possible because of another invention of his, the Mobius strip antenna. Now a Mobius strip, mathematicians will tell you, is an actual geometric possibility that can be demonstrated and created. Utilizing such a principle, Om declared, would afford "infinite wave length" to the antenna, and the power received could be in any quantity, depending upon the size and capacity of the "Augmenter," which, in turn, was connected to a "Cosmon," a large, strange-looking tube inside which electrical discharges crackled when he pulled a switch. So far he had been able to power an ordinary light bulb, but when further developed the device could furnish power for the entire house. All of which was a trifle unethical, however, he explained, for the power was being robbed from the outputs of radio and television transmitters.

Then he cackled sadistically as he pictured how the engineer at the transmitter would see the indicator needle fluctuate, and how he then would apply more power. All this was told so graphically I could almost visualize the harassed engineer, getting a case of ulcers after a day or two of coping with Om's "Electrocosmeter," as he labeled the device.

Though his guests laugh heartily all through each performance, a visit to Om's basement becomes almost disquieting at times. Isolated from the noise of the city streets, the guest is almost projected into another world. Amid Om's crackling and humming devices the visitor often experiences a momentary suspension of disbelief, a brief doubt that all he is seeing and hearing is a joke. One wonders if some of the devices might actually work, and if Om, after all, is pulling one's leg.

Om also fiddles with old cars, and often enlists his brother Dom in the search for missing parts.

Dom must have lost the Curilovic Report, he told Roberts, when he went to the West End Auto Wreckers to pick up some parts for his brother.

Yet Lucchesi couldn't entirely believe he had lost it.

"You know, Augie, that I don't go around losing things. And

if I lost the report, why didn't I lose the other mail as well? If someone stole it out of the car, why didn't they take this money?" and he held up an envelope containing a five dollar bill.

Lucchesi picked up the phone and dialed the Hudson County Police. He asked for Lieutenant Kellegher.

He also got the runaround. The lieutenant was off duty that day, and why didn't he call back the next day.

Lucchesi thought for a moment, figured they should let things develop over the weekend and see what happened. The next day would be Saturday, when he was due at the factory to consult with a fellow from Louisiana who was flying in. He and Roberts could go to the station together on Monday, he suggested.

It did look as if they were getting the old runaround procedure, Roberts remarked. Why? You would expect the police to think the men whose names were on the report were a bunch of harmless crackpots, for at that time people generally pooh-poohed saucers and laughed at anyone who believed in them.

Lucchesi and Roberts visited the Hudson County Police together on Monday morning, and again talked with the desk sergeant. They asked if Lieutenant Kellegher was available.

The sergeant was sorry, Lieutenant Kellegher was on a case, but what did their inquiry refer to.

Lucchesi wasn't to be dismissed easily. He reviewed the story: how Roberts had received the phone call, how Kellegher had said he actually possessed the missing report.

The desk sergeant became noticeably flustered.

"I tell you, I'll just give Kellegher a buzz. I happen to know where he's working."

He called Kellegher, asked him about the report, engaged him in lengthy conversation. They thought it was unusual that the sergeant listened most of the time, holding his hand over the receiver as if in an effort to prevent their hearing what was being said.

The sergeant would say, "Yes," "Uh-huh," "Right." At one time he said "No, he didn't."

Then Lucchesi and Roberts received a digest of the conversation. Kellegher hadn't found any report, nor had he telephoned anyone about it. He knew nothing at all of the matter.

But it seemed as if the desk sergeant didn't want them to leave the station right away. He suggested they go back down to the record room, where Roberts had been before. He didn't give them any good reason, but they went there as directed. Detective King wasn't present at the time, but he came rushing in, and seemed to be trying to stall them. They thought they could detect a worried look on his face.

"King didn't act curious," Lucchesi commented on a tape recording describing the sequence of events. "And a cop without curiosity is out of character. Have you ever seen a cop who wasn't curious?

Realizing they were getting nowhere they decided to go to their own precinct and see Inspector Foley, chief of detectives there. Lucchesi thought it would also be wise to lay the matter before Jack Brewster, a local FBI agent whom he knew personally and whose office was in the same building.

On their way they noticed a Hudson County police car speeding toward the station. That was somewhat odd, Lucchesi decided later, for on their way to the station he had seen the same car, with the same man behind the wheel, tearing away from the station. Could this have been the evasive Lieutenant Kellegher returning to handle the situation in person? Was that the reason for the obvious stall?

When they arrived at their own precinct station Brewster was out, but Inspector Foley, usually gruff and busy, broke his pattern and took time to listen patiently to the whole matter. He suggested they return the next day and talk to Brewster.

That wasn't necessary. Roberts excitedly telephoned Lucchesi the next day. While he was out on an assignment a police car had driven up to his house and delivered a letter to his sister. It was addressed to Roberts, from "Dept. of Police, County of Hudson, Newark Turnpike at Hackensack Bridge, Postoffice Box No. 54, Five Corner Station JC8, New Jersey."

The envelope also bore the notation, "Found by patrolman Thomas Keenan."

It contained the missing report.

Was all this on the level, my colleagues asked each other, and had they used their imaginations too freely? Maybe they still had enough of the juvenile in them to enjoy making a mystery out of a quite ordinary affair.

But somehow it seemed to tie in with my own visit from the FBI, of which I had informed them.

A few days later we would wonder if it did not also tie in with strange happenings in Bridgeport, Connecticut.

VII

Bridgeport, Connecticut

I couldn't for the life of me figure out Bender's letter of September 16, 1953. The beginning was routine enough. He thought the special article concerning the activities of the Department of Investigation, which I had prepared for publication in *Space Review*, was excellent, though he preferred to change the last line which stated the FBI had visited me.

"I thought it proper," Bender wrote, "to change that line to read, 'members of the United States Government have paid a visit to IFSB just recently.'"

The mysterious part of his letter was the third paragraph.

"I do not know if I advised you or not, but do not accept any more memberships until after the October issue of *Space Review* is in your hands."

Did Bender plan some change in the organization? True, it was growing by leaps and bounds. It now had representatives in nearly all the 48 states, branches in five foreign countries. Maybe, I thought, he had found it necessary to reorganize in some fashion, in order to handle operations on the larger scale now possible and necessary.

My mind flashed back to the April, 1953, issue of the quarterly publication in which the staff stated "A STARTLING REVELATION BY OUR PRESIDENT" would be published in the next number. No revelation of such anticipated nature had appeared in the next issue, that of July, 1953, to my knowledge, and that was strange, I reflected.

Then Bender's letter, come to think of it, didn't sound right. It was formal, stilted, not like Bender at all. Since we had become very good friends through the mail, our letters were quite informal, contained many references of personal nature. This one sounded odd, if only because of its abrupt, businesslike manner.

I was to get the shock of my life when I received a tape-recorded message from Lucchesi and plugged in my recorder expecting to hear a routine communication.

A saucer researcher without a tape recorder is considered almost a nonentity by those who ponder the elusive disks. He is like a diplomat without evening clothes, a chef without a white cap.

A recorder is a camera for speech. If you interview someone who has had an unusual experience, listen later and you can track down every faltering word, analyze the tone of the voice, and pick up many facets of the personality you would otherwise pass over. In long distance discussions about saucers between exponents of the movement recorders are invaluable. You can talk much faster than you can type a letter, as Carolyn, my secretary, busy for an entire day transcribing Lucchesi's tape, complained petulantly.

I can get my message across far more naturally and fluently if I can sit down and talk into a tape recorder. In writing I often am in a hurry and skip over important details.

I could probably sum up Lucchesi's tape letter in a page or two, but I'd like to share the entire thing with you if I may. I wish you were sitting here in my office and could hear it all, as Lucchesi intoned it into the microphone soon after it had happened, while the amazing details were fresh in his mind. Since you can't hear it, I'm going to include it just as he spoke it, with some uninteresting personal references eliminated. If this is not great literature, forgive both him and me, for it is written as it was spoken, informally, from friend to friend.

❀ ❀ ❀ ❀ ❀

This is a talking letter, from Dominick C. Lucchesi, 74 Booraem Avenue, Jersey City, New Jersey, to Gray Barker, Box 2228, Clarksburg, West Virginia.

Hello, Gray:

I will begin by telling you what happened this morning (noise)—I'm moving my chair over here by my desk and am adjusting the volume as I speak—so I hope it doesn't sound too bad.

This morning I listened to the tape you sent to me. I always enjoy listening to tapes, and on your latest one I enjoyed particularly the information you gave me about Shaver. But after listening to the tape, I hated to part with it, so I am using a different type of tape on which to reply (Author's note: "Tape respondents," as such correspondents are known, usually reply on the same tapes they receive from other parties, simply erasing the former messages. Thus few new blank tapes need be purchased in order to pursue this kind of "writing."—G.B.).

I enjoyed the sound effects you had on your tape, and the jokes about the bodies, and I thought I'd kid around by starting off my reply with some kind of weird sound effect, since my brother, Om, has an electronics laboratory downstairs, and has often helped me to record strange sounds on tapes I have sent out, such as echoes and the like, electronically, mechanically and otherwise. But due to the fact that Om is out now and that I'm all alone in the house, it is quite difficult for me to do it alone, since you have to make a lot of electrical connections on his recording apparatus, and I'm not too familiar with his equipment.

But actually, Gray, *some very interesting things have happened,* and the only way I can describe these to you is by using tape.

As far as my being investigated by anyone is concerned, no one that I know of has interrogated Augie (Roberts) or myself—unless it might have been someone with whom we are well acquainted, and whom we might not have realized was an investigator of one type or another.

It all began when Augie bought a new car last week. I worked on it for him Saturday, making some adjustments they had missed at the sales agency.

The next day being a Sunday Augie said he'd like to try the car out on a long trip, and we decided to drive up to Bridgeport and see Al (Bender). As you know it's only about 75 or 80 miles, and takes only about two hours to get there. And with the pressure of work as it is now it is quite relaxing to be able to get out of town now and then and enjoy a nice drive on Sunday. So I telephoned Al from my home and asked him if he would be there and he said he would.

On the way Augie's car overheated, probably due to a blocked radiator, and we decided it would be more practical to turn back, since the overheating might easily damage the engine which had not yet been broken in. We went back to Augie's house from there; we were about—oh, say about 40 blocks from it when the trouble occurred. Augie called Al from his house, telling him we wouldn't be able to get there.

Augie asked Al if there was anything new in "saucerology," as he put it.

You'll have to excuse the hesitation between words, Gray. I'm not accustomed to making what might be termed "tape letters," and have a very strange feeling, here, talking to myself, so to speak.

What I'm actually doing is making believe you're in the chair in front of me, and that I'm speaking to you.

This is all very hard to describe, about Al, that is, for actually the conversation was not between Al and myself, but between him and Augie. Actually the phone call lasted for about 20 to 25 minutes and Augie and I had been thinking previously about the strange silence from Al regarding saucers—his lack of correspondence. So Augie questioned him as to what recent events had occurred since he had written.

To make a long story short, Gray, I can't give it to you word for word, what had happened is something like this:

Al told Augie that *Space Review* WOULD come out on October 15, but whether it would come out after that was something else.

It seems something strange has occurred in IFSB.

Well, Augie was quite persistent, and kept pushing Al for more information. Finally Al stated bluntly, "I know the secret of the disks!"

He added that *three men had visited him, and in effect shut him up completely as far as saucer investigation is concerned!*

Now the way I gather it, Al had run across something important during his study of the saucer mystery. This information was evidently the solution to the mystery. In his position as head of the IFSB he is in what one might picture as a vortex, at its very bottom, the focal point for all the saucer information being run down by the hundreds of IFSB members. He had run across the secret unexpectedly while going through all this material.

Al also said that the remaining copies of *Space Review*—he had kept 15 copies of each back issue—had been confiscated. Augie asked Al if he or I, that is Augie or myself, would be able to find out the same thing that Al had found out by studying what saucer data we had on hand. Al said, "Yes," but that he was pledged to secrecy, on his honor as an American citizen not to speak about the actual thing that he knew.

In other words, Al told Augie that *he knows what the saucers are!*

And that *the three men pledged him to silence!*

Augie asked Al if he should continue with his photographs and other methods of research which would assist in the solution of the problem, and Al said for Augie not to waste his time or money delving deeper into the saucer mystery.

I have not mentioned to Augie that I am sending this tape to you, because I think he is quite frightened.

But as you said in your tape, "we are doing nothing wrong," unless you want to call curiosity a bad trait. After all, curiosity is what makes people delve into the unknown and come up with things which are benefits to humanity, and represent progress.

Anyway, Gray, that's it. I really can't say much about it. I spoke to Al briefly myself, but didn't mention any of the things Augie was discussing, for after all, I feel that if someone has a secret I will not push him to tell me—that is entirely up to him. And I wouldn't respect him if he did, if he had pledged his secrecy as an American citizen.

Anyway, I know that your inquisitive mind will certainly like to hear this. In fact, you may already have heard about it. Whether you have or not, I do not know. I'm lighting a cigarette, Gray, excuse me a minute (pause).

The issues of *Space Review* the men confiscated are, as you know, in wide circulation, so why they were taken is beyond my comprehension. Logically it does not seem proper.

There is something that smells to me in this whole business, Gray. Al doesn't say they were government men who visited him, but his mentioning his pledge as an American citizen seems to indicate such.

Somehow these men do not seem to me to be from the government. If they were, the way Al talks I would believe that some rights of American citizens are being infringed upon. I do not think I'm speaking out of turn when I say this.

He did not reveal what branch of the government they were from—if they were from the government at all.

Augie and I probably will go to see Al next Sunday. Let me see, today, I believe, is September 29.

Now, Gray, I would like your opinion on just what you think has happened. If you know something, I don't like to be left hanging in mid-air. Al is a very good friend of mine and I know he would not do this if he did not have to. Maybe it was because he was afraid to speak freely over the phone but it looks as if he could have hinted a little more than he did.

I have studied issues 1, 2 and 3 of *Space Review* diligently. I've known for some time that Al, in the next issue, supposed to come out on October 15, was going to reveal something of great importance. What it was, not having seen Al for quite a while, I do not know.

Probably if I had gone to see Al before this happened he would have told me, as he usually does when we visit him, what would be in the next issue, for he is always very enthusiastic about forthcoming numbers of the publication.

Gray, from Augie's conversation with him, and my own impressions upon hearing his voice during this telephone call, it seems a great change has come over Al.

It appears he has lost all the interest and enthusiasm that used to seem to set him on fire—so to speak—now that he evidently *knows*.

Logically, I have come to six possible conclusions as to what he found out, but I realize that doesn't help much. I have at least, I believe, narrowed the possibilities down to six, and that should be of some value. Lacking enough data, I am unable to narrow it to fewer ramifications.

These possibilities are, and I will read them off my notes as I have them outlined:

(1) The saucers come from space.

(2) The saucers represent American secret defense weapons.

(3) The saucers represent secret devices built by a foreign power.

(4) The saucers represent a kind of fourth dimension, and are not solid or real as we would think of it.

(5) The saucers are coming from a secret place on the

Earth itself, constructed by a people we do not know about.

(6) Bender found out that we have already achieved space travel, have already launched an artificial satellite, or, more fantastic but possible, that *man is already on the Moon.*

Some things in these past issues of *Space Review* I have been going through seem to strike me, things published in copies confiscated by the three men.

I call your attention to Vol. 1, No. 1, page 3: Al, in his editorial, states, "In my opinion, the U. S. A. has already sent a rocket to the moon with humans as passengers, but under strict secrecy. The general public won't know about it for a couple of years. It would be dangerous to reveal this to the public now, since one of the foreign powers is in a position to wage war or challenge us. In summing up, it would be wise for the public to start turning its eyes and thoughts toward the heavens, because there is more danger lurking there than on the earth itself."

Or, in Vol. 2, No. 1, the conclusion of the article by Rev. S. L. Daw: "The United States may be experimenting with something that the public is not aware of, and it is doing its best to keep it a secret. The age of the rocket ship is just around the corner."

Do you suppose Al could have chanced upon some of our plans for space travel and that this information involved strict security?

The way Al talked to Augie, it sounded as if something horrible might be going to take place. Look up the editorial in Vol. 2, No. 2, wherein Al is discussing the possibility that the Earth might capsize due to the accumulation of ice at the South Pole:

"The time for the next capsizing may be 1953 and from all points of view, the earth is 'pretty wobbly' and that time may be at hand. Saucers from other planets have been sighted, more so now than at any other time in our history. The coming of the saucers may have to do with saving us from our horrible fate."

If the saucers are real and are about to land, I am wondering if your own article, in the same issue, could represent an answer to the question of why Al closed up; the article in which you asked, "What if the entire structures of our religions should be shattered to bits upon the first interview with a little man who gets out of a spinning space ship?"

In going over Vol. 2, No. 1 again, Gray, I cannot help but detect a similarity between Al's conversation with Augie and a statement made by George D. Fawcett, of the IFSB International Council, on Page 11. He says:

"I have just decided to stop the investigation that I began a little over five years ago on one of the most fascinating mysteries of modern times, that being the well known 'Flying Saucer' phenomena."

But the end of the article is even more interesting. "Regardless, the future will tell! In closing I'd like to use a favorite phrase of Charlie Lineberry, Lynchburg College student who said, 'things are really looking up.' I wonder if some things aren't looking DOWN, too. . . ."

What I'm getting at, that "down" is in big print, and I know that sounds fantastic.

That, by the way, is another mysterious thing Al said to Augie. "The truth," Al said, "is *fantastic.*" That was all he could tell him, and naturally we may find out more when we visit him.

Now I might be thinking in the wrong channels, but actually the way the man began that article is how Al now speaks—about giving up the investigation, though it was only natural to give up when someone *knows* the answer.

Now—that "looking DOWN" business. Could that have been a hint? Could that have been what Al found out? Was he thinking, possibly, in a Shaverian sense? I think you can understand what I mean, knowing some of the inside on the Shaver mystery. I don't know if you have the issue of *Amazing Stories*, containing nothing except the Shaver mystery compiled in that one number—or maybe it was a hard cover book—but I believe Al has that particular number.

Maybe Al tied in certain events which were stated in that issue by Shaver, such as pertaining to actual entrances to the underworld Shaver swears actually exists. If you will notice, Shaver does claim there are entrances down around your territory, particularly in Virginia, around the Smoky Mountains and that area. And if you take notice, many saucer sightings have occurred in that area of the United States.

Gray, other people may hear this tape, through one way or another.

It is not impossible that you, yourself, might be an agent. That is something which is irrelevant, and I am completely indifferent to the possibility. My address is known. Anyone wishing to contact me may always find me here. So any agent who hears this tape and consequently wishes to contact me can do so at 74 Booraem Avenue, Jersey City, New Jersey.

Well, that's over with, Gray.

Al said that they, the three men, more or less *edited* the copy he will use in the next issue of *Space Review*. So I am looking forward to receiving that issue, to seeing how badly butchered the truth will likely be.

If curiosity is a crime, well then I'm willing to stop being curious. I would not want to be delving into something that would in any way endanger the security of our cities and of

119

our country as a whole. And if this is the case, I wish a person of authority would approach me and tell me so. But until that time I am going to continue to be curious and explore this thing for the answer I am sure I can arrive at, if Al has been able to do so.

Unless you, or Al, or someone who I know is not a fool can show me that I am wrong in this statement.

There *has* been a silence from your end, also, so you probably have been approached and told to keep quiet, but I doubt it—unless you have discovered something which would make you in the know. All of us can advance theories, but the one thing that is difficult to advance is fact.

I intend to keep investigating these phenomena and I would like your opinion, and to know just what you are going to do, whether you have been approached.

As I said, I haven't seen Augie since we talked with Al, which means he is in a state of confusion or even fright. Probably he is trying to figure the entire thing out and decide whether or not he should go ahead trying to find a solution.

Al told him that collecting data and photographs was entirely useless now. However, I wouldn't interpret that as meaning one would get into trouble doing so. Even if Al is no longer interested in finding out more, he should remember that such research is still very important to those who yet do not know the truth.

I suspect Augie will be over some time today, however, for he has been away an unusually long time. Normally he comes over to compare information almost every day.

Now that Al will not be publishing *Space Review,* I see no reason why I should not offer the material I have written for it to you. Perhaps you would like to use some of this in *The*

Saucerian. Al said I "might just as well forget about" my drawings, the same way Augie is supposed to forget about his photographs. But I cannot see it that way, Gray. As you know, I do some drafting in my spare time. I have on hand complete mechanical drawings for a saucer. I have included every "angle." Everything is figured, mechanically, aerodynamically and otherwise. The drawings are concise and clear, and if you would like to see them, I would be glad to mail them to you, since it seems Al will have no interest in looking at them.

Just because Bender is out of action doesn't mean *we* are knocked out, because the more we push the quicker they are going to bring it out into the light and let everybody know.

We don't have the *key*, that's our only trouble. But if Al found it, *we* can find it. We have a clue in the fact they confiscated the back issues of *Space Review*. There must be something in those issues!

I believe we must look for something *fantastic*, for that is just how Al put it about what he had learned.

The way Augie quoted Al, he said, "I went into the fantastic and came up with the answer." Now what I want to know, just what is *"fantastic"*? Does he mean he went into the spiritual end of it, the spiritual world? Of course what might be fantastic to one person could be ordinary to another, depending upon his past experiences and mental conditioning. To some people space travel in itself would be fantastic.

That seems to be the story on Al, Gray. As much as I know of it.

The question now is this: what should we do about it? Do you wish to try and get at the bottom of it, or are you, by chance, now in the same position as Al?

If you have been visited, and if you have been shut up, I

am not asking you to tell me what you know, or found out. Just send a tape back to me discussing general things, and I'll know that *you* know. If this is the case I hope such a situation will not interrupt the pleasant personal relationship we have enjoyed. After all there are many other subjects in which we have common interests, and there is no reason why we cannot discuss them.

We are awaiting your opinion before we take any further action. As I said, we plan to go to Bridgeport Sunday. Do you think this is wise? If we do go, what line of questioning should we use in finding out more from Al? I think, from the conversation with Al, it would be wiser if you put your answer on a tape. Al fears his telephone is tapped.

So long, Gray. I am looking forward to hearing from you.

*   *   *   *   *

The reels of the tape recorder continued to revolve, as I sat there, amazed and dumbfounded. The tape ran out and the "flap! flap! flap!" of the take-up reel pulled me out of my abstraction, and I turned off the machine.

This was IT! There must be something *very very* real to the saucer mystery!

The way it looked, any minute there might be a knock on my own door!

I wondered just how I would react. The three men presumably had shaken Al Bender badly.

Were they from the government? If they were, there must be some very funny things going on in Washington, things one would not like to hear about. It looked as if the saucer situation had come to the point where even the government was scared.

I could see a dim picture slowly revolving and then coming into mental focus. The U. S. A. in a day which might not be far in the future, a day that might already be upon us. The secret of the saucers was out, and the answer was so fantastic the mind of the average citizen, imbued with the delusion that he was alone in the universe, had snapped!

The clergy had charged him to look up only for angels, and now he saw physical beings in the heavens. Were the beings in the saucers men, or gods? Or demons?

The government had declared martial law in an effort to quell the panic.

Already here might be an indication that just such a state of affairs was expected—soon. For here was a man, his home entered, and his organization, heretofore more of a hobby than a cause, shattered to bits. Whoever the three men were, they didn't want him to think any longer, or to encourage others to think.

At that moment I knew I had to get to the bottom of it. At that moment I began to realize the most vital aspect of the saucer mystery.

More important than what the saucers are, where they come from and why they are here is a glaring question mark:

What are the *people* going to think about the disks?

How will they react to them?

I shuddered at the consideration.

Mankind would be in a mess, believes psychologist C. G. Jung, who made a statement about saucers.

"We would be placed in the very questionable position of today's primitive societies that clash with the superior cultures of the white race. All initiative would be wrested from us. As an old witch doctor once said to me, with tears in his eyes: We would 'have no more dreams.'

"Our science and technology would go on the junk pile. What such a catastrophe would mean morally we can gauge only by the pitiful decline of primitive cultures that has taken place before our eyes."

We hope that when and if the time comes for a disk to land in Times Square, to formally herald the New Age, the creatures inside, if humanoid, will not share our human natures.

For if they do, they may send missionaries among us.

VIII

Return to Bridgeport

You fiddle with your recorder, wondering how you should answer Lucchesi.

If things are as bad as they look, you, yourself, will receive a visit soon. If the callers are from the government, and appeal to you as a citizen, you will have no alternative other than to submit to the conspiracy of silence, for they likely know the best course, have arrived at their conclusion only after long, careful thought.

But somehow when you think about it you wish you could

puke. You know a lot of people like yourself are clamoring for the answer. Somehow you feel the truth should be allowed to stand on its own two feet, that the people, the little people, who would be on the receiving end of a possible invasion from space or some great catastrophe the saucers were here to prevent, should be told.

But what if you were in the position of making that decision? Would you tell them?

I mulled it over in my mind. It would take some thinking, consideration of every contingency. Maybe that was why the people hadn't been told: the government was unable to decide, one way or the other. No, I wouldn't relish having such a responsibility on my shoulders.

I jerked the electric cord from the wall, threw it across the recorder. Then I went out for a drink. Half way around the block I turned around, came back into the office and telephoned Bender.

I might learn something he would not tell Lucchesi or Roberts. Anyway, it was worth a try. It couldn't hurt anything. And I might learn something.

I didn't.

Bender didn't sound natural. He acted as if he didn't want to talk to me. I asked him to confirm what I heard from Lucchesi and Roberts.

"What they told you is true. I know what the saucers are."

I pressed him for additional details.

About all I could get from him were statements such as "I can't answer that," or "I don't care to comment further."

I asked him if the three men were from the government. He couldn't answer that either. I asked him if my own visit from the FBI or the matter of the lost report had anything to do with his own troubles. He said there was no connection, as far as he knew.

I did draw from him an unusual attitude, for Bender, who formerly was enthusiastic about saucer research:

"The saucers don't interest me any more. I've lost all interest in them."

"Was that because," I asked, "you found out they were too ordinary to be interesting (I was hinting they might have turned out to be government devices), or that what you discovered about them is painful for you to think about?"

"The latter," he said, with a detectable hint of fright in his voice.

Bender said he was sorry he couldn't tell more, hinted that as a friend I should press him no further. As soon as he was permitted to talk I would be one of the first to receive the complete details, he said.

I hung up and telephoned Lucchesi. He wasn't at home, so I got in touch with Roberts.

I went over the thing with him.

"First of all, Augie, have no fear. I've not been 'shushed up,' nor am I any kind of government investigator."

I told him I was just as puzzled as he and Dom.

It was important, I remember telling him, to get to Bender personally. Maybe matters he feared to discuss over the phone might be given out were some of us there, on a personal visit. I suggested he and Lucchesi drive to Connecticut as planned the following Sunday. Although I planned to come East soon, I would be unable to get away from the office that coming weekend because of some theatre problems.

"The important thing to remember, Augie, is this: you must remember everything that is said."

"I'm sure he wouldn't let us set up a tape recorder," Roberts said, "if he's afraid to talk over the phone."

"I don't mean a tape recorder; I mean notes."

"But I can't have a note pad in my hand. It would give the whole thing away!"

"Not in your *hand,* old boy. You must find an excuse to get away from Al and Dom now and then, and write down everything that is said while it is fresh in your mind."

"But what sort of an excuse?"

"Now, Augie, I'm surprised at you. It's elementary. There's surely a john in the house. Tell Al you took a laxative, or that you are having some kind of bowel trouble. Run out every fifteen minutes and scribble like mad. When we get those notes maybe we can put it all together and come up with something."

Roberts remonstrated he was a poor actor, but said he would try.

"If you think you can't make it look real, *take one!*

"Take what?"

"A *laxative,* you idiot!"

* * * * *

I never asked Roberts how far he had to go to make his excuses convincing. But he came up with the notes.

He and Lucchesi drove to Bridgeport as planned, found Bender friendly and hospitable as usual, but strangely shaken, it seemed.

After all, Lucchesi reasoned later, a number of causes may have contributed to his upset condition. Besides learning something obviously unpleasant about saucers, Bender had been told to stop investigating them, and to close his large organization. The IFSB had been to him a dream almost fulfilled. And now it burst, like a bubble, and he had to scrap it.

The notes Roberts took are not entirely verbatim, but they are close to what actually was said. They may sound informal because they have not been edited, and may even contain grammatical errors. For they are quoted almost as they were spoken.

If Bender's rejoinder, "I can't answer that," sounds repetitive, forgive us. For that was the reply to many of the questions, and we list all of the queries for complete reference.

The Bender mystery is not solved. I have collected reams of notes about it. I could write two books like this one filled with theories and data I cannot publish here because of space limitations and other reasons.

I have always felt if I could organize these notes into some kind of readable whole and distribute these findings widely, somewhere there would be someone in whose mind they would sound an inspired tinkle. One little idea from a reader may be the final key to unlocking the entire mystery. Then someone, who has had a similar experience, may read it and realize someone else had the same troubles. He may talk.

Roberts does not record who asked specific questions, he or Lucchesi, nor does it matter. Both quizzed Bender.

I hope you will read carefully this account of one of the world's strangest quiz programs, which took place October 4, 1953, in Bender's home, a program never broadcast nor telecast, a show in which the only prize was $64,000 worth of confusion.

Q. When did the three men visit you?

A. I can't answer that.

Q. Who were the men?

129

A. I can't answer that.

Q. Were they from the government?

A. I can't answer that.

Q. Do saucers come from space?

A. I can't answer that.

Q. Are the saucers real; are they made of something solid?

A. I can't answer that.

Q. Does it have anything to do with the space platform?

A. I can't answer that.

Q. Can you tell me where you found your source of information?

A. I was turning a theory over and over in my mind. When I got some actual names and places to back it up I submitted it to someone. Then the men came.

Q. Who was that "someone" you mention?

A. I can't answer that.

Q. Does it have anything at all to do with the Shaver Mystery?

A. No answer at all (Bender tensed noticeably when asked).

Q. Is the flying saucer going to be a help to the world?

A. It's going to be both good and bad.

Q. Are saucers going to harm us in any way?

A. I can't answer that.

Q. What do you think of Shaver? Is there anything to his stories?

A. No answer; Bender changed the subject.

Q. Do you think it will be safe for me to go on the skywatch tower all alone at night?

A. It would be safer (Roberts believes Bender probably meant to say it would be safer on the tower than it would be on the ground).

Q. Are all of us who are trying to find out what the saucers are about going to get into trouble over it?

A. I don't believe so.

Q. Will Gray, Dom and I get into trouble over what you found out? Did we have anything to do with giving you a clue?

A. No, to both questions.

Q. Does the government know about saucers?

A. They have known what they are for two years.

Q. Will they tell the people what they are?

A. It has got to a point where they will have to.

Q. When will the government tell the people about the saucers?

A. If not within five months from now, not for about four years.

Q. Is it going to be frightening to a lot of people?

A. If people like you and me have an idea what saucers are, and expect something unusual and fantastic, think what will happen when it is suddenly told to people who are totally unprepared.

Q. Do we have any defense for it?

A. No.

Q. Can we stop what is going to happen?

A. Just as the three men who paid me a visit were leaving, one of them lingered for a moment and said, "In our government we have the smartest men in the country. They can't find a defense for it. How can *you* do anything about it?"

Q. In that case I'll buy myself a good gun.

A. That won't help you much.

Q. Can it be stopped by a bullet?

A. I can't answer that.

Q. Why can't you talk freely about this thing?

A. Just before the men left one of them said, "I suppose you know you're on your honor as an American. If I hear another word out of your office you're in trouble."

Q. What will they do with you if you give out information?

A. Put me in jail and keep me shut up.

Q. Would they put *me* in jail if I found out and told?

A. Yes.

Q. At home do I have the answer as to what the saucers are?

A. I'm quite sure you do.

Q. Can you tell me where to look for the answers?

A. I can't tell you that.

Q. How did you find out about it? Can't you tell me just where you got your theory?

A. All I can say is this: It was something that I was thinking about for a long time. I went into the fantastic and came up with the answer.

Q. How did the three men find out about your theory?

A. I wrote about it and was going to have it printed. I sent it to a friend of mine, and right after that the three men paid me a visit. They had my story with them.

Q. Were the men friendly with you?

A. They were pretty rough with me. Two men did all the talking, and the other kept watching me all the time they were here. He didn't take his eyes off me.

Q. Did you notice what the men wore?

A. They wore the same type of clothes and hats. Dark clothes and black hats.

Q. Did they make any comments about the size of IFSB?

A. One of them went over to the map on the wall, saw all the pins denoting locations of IFSB representatives, and said, "God, but you're all over the place!"

Q. What else did they do in your office besides talk?

A. They took the serial numbers of my tape recorders.

Q. Do they know about Gray, Dom and me?

A. They had all of your addresses and details about you with them with the papers they had in their hands.

Q. Do the saucers have life in them?

A. I can't answer that.

Q. Do the saucers come from Venus as stated in Adamski's book?

A. I can't answer that.

Q. Do they come from Mars?

A. I can't answer that.

Q. I would like to write a story to sell to a magazine. Can you give me a good subject to write about? (This question was asked in the hope of obtaining some clue.)

A. Here is something no one has used before. Suppose there was another world out in space, and there the people were black. What do you think would happen if they came to this planet? Do you think they would help the colored or the white people? You know the prejudices that exist here, and if they came to Earth, what do you think would happen? It would make a good story, don't you think?

Q. What will happen to the world when the people find out about the saucers?

A. There are going to be quite a few changes, in all things.

Q. Will it affect science?

A. It is going to put a big dent in it.

Q. Are you making any long-range plans, say for about five years from now?

A. Yes.

Q. Then the world isn't going to come to an end?

A. No answer. Subject was changed to the ice caps at the South Pole.

Q. Do you think the world will fall over if the ice keeps accumulating?

A. I don't know.

Q. Has the South Pole anything to do with saucers?

A. I can't answer that.

Q. There are only half a dozen things I can think of right now to explain the saucers: Out of space, something to do with a space platform, some government on Earth owns it, Shaver was right, it's in the ocean, it could be a time machine. Or it may very well be that the United States has reached the Moon.

A. You forgot about natural phenomena.

Q. Do you mean the saucers are life themselves? If so I can't believe that. I saw one last year, and it was a solid aircraft of some kind.

A. I can't answer that.

Q. You say you know what the saucers are. Do they look like what I saw and described to you last year?

A. I can't answer that.

Q. Do the saucers you know about look like what everybody else is seeing?

A. I can't answer that.

Q. Why do you delay answering each of my questions for a few seconds?

A. I'm afraid of slipping; if I do I can get into a lot of trouble.

Q. With this information you claim to know about the saucers, if you did write about it, and had it published, what would happen?

A. I would likely go down in history. Also I would go to jail for quite a long time.

Q. Can you tell me why I can't continue what I'm doing about saucers? You told me to stop wasting my time with them, and to stop spending my money on research.

A. I can't answer that.

Q. If I keep going to the skywatch tower with my camera, will I be able to get another picture of a saucer?

A. You might.

Q. Was the saucer I photographed last year real? Did I prove its reality to you?

A. I can't answer that.

Q. Will it affect all of our lives?

A. There will be changes in everybody's life.

Q. You said the three men who paid you the visit were pretty rough with you. Can you tell me just what you meant by that?

A. They were not too friendly.

IX

Maury Island

As I pondered over the notes of the interview I was at once excited and disappointed.

Excited because it looked as if something really big had happened in Bridgeport, something that indicated the saucer mystery had almost reached a stage of precipitation, when all the clues would fall together into a meaningful whole, condense into a concrete solution.

I was disappointed because the interview, though I was convinced it was packed with meaning, only added to my confusion.

In the back of my mind gnawed another disquieting thought.

136

If Bender was pledged to secrecy, surely he would have given Roberts and Lucchesi no information, if he could help it, that would reveal the secret. Maybe he was deliberately trying to confuse us, putting us on the wrong track.

But I was sure that somewhere Bender had slipped. I could feel it. But I couldn't put my finger on it.

Then, what about the drawing? Bender, in a phone conversation with Roberts, had let slip that the three men "would not like it," though now it was already off the press and distributed to my subscribers.

The drawing had been completed before Bender was shut up.

Small amateur publications, such as *The Saucerian*, cannot afford to purchase art work from professionals. Their publishers must depend upon volunteering amateurs to illustrate their magazines, unless they are artists themselves.

I can't draw even a straight line, and when I bend myself to the task of drawing a picture, results are disastrous.

Bender had volunteered to draw a cover illustration for me, and came through with it shortly before his mysterious bout with the visitors.

And whether the three men liked it or not, it was on the November, 1953 issue, already in the hands of my readers.

Had Bender consciously or subconsciously put some of the theory he had evolved into the illustration, Lucchesi wondered, as he tried to analyze just what it pictured. Dom couldn't decide whether the strange scene, picturing a large construction rising from a crater, with saucers using its apex for a landing base, represented a scene on the moon, some other planet, or on the earth.

When we asked Bender if the drawing had any significance, he gave a reply now familiar to you, "I can't answer that."

Whether or not the art work had been inadvisable, Bender wanted nothing further to do with *The Saucerian*. He had been listed on the editorial page as "Eastern Editor." He asked me to remove his name from the masthead, expressing regret that he could at that time offer no further services to my publication.

But there remained another source of information. The last issue of *Space Review* to represent the IFSB officially would contain an announcement of some kind about the organization's demise. The three men had told Bender what to say, and edited the copy.

Finally it arrived in the mail.

It contained a statement about the IFSB's closing, and a form for members to return for refunds on subscriptions, along with two cryptic items.

"LATE BULLETIN. A source, which the IFSB considers very reliable, has informed us that the investigation of the flying-saucer mystery and the solution is approaching its final stages.

"This same source to whom we had preferred data, which had come into our possession, suggested that it was not the proper method and time to publish this data in *Space Review*."

The other item:

"STATEMENT OF IMPORTANCE. The mystery of the flying saucers is no longer a mystery. The source is already known, but any information about this is being withheld by orders from a higher source. We would like to print the full story in *Space Review*, but because of the nature of the information we are very sorry that we have been advised in the negative.

"We advise those engaged in saucer work to please be **very** cautious."

If we were to solve what we now termed the "Bender mystery," it looked as if we would have to seek research avenues other than the last issue of *Space Review.*

It only added further to our confusion. For example, the last line, "*We advise those engaged in saucer work to please be very cautious.*"

Cautious of what? The three men who might visit us? Or would there be repercussions from the saucers themselves—were we to be cautious of the saucer people?

And always that gnawing question: had Bender deliberately tried to get us off the track? He hinted that when we learned what he did we would be "very greatly surprised."

Maybe the visitors were not from the government after all! Would it be too fantastic to consider the possibility of a visit from space people themselves? Surely. But if the saucers did come from space, that consideration could be no more fantastic than the appearance of the saucers.

Could some terrestrial organization, unconnected with government, at least officially, be going to fantastic lengths to keep the mystery permanently a mystery?

Whoever or whatever visited Bender had deeply impressed him, and greatly frightened him.

Later on, when I continued my investigations into similar avenues I was to find that for some reason a man will not talk after one of these visitations.

When such a person is approached, whoever tells the person to shut up does so in such a way or imparts such terrifying information that the man on the receiving end is scared almost out of his wits!

How? Why?

The October, 1953, issue of *Space Review* made my mind up

for me. I would do everything in my power to get to the bottom of just what was going on. Since then I have collected a filing cabinet full of information, gathered at the odd moments I have had available, aside from my business, for saucer research.

I now believe those pieces of information are beginning to coalesce.

I was in a good position to attack the problem. I had readers throughout the United States and in many foreign countries. These readers would send me any saucer information coming into their hands or conduct on-the-spot investigations for me. My readers seemed to be more than subscribers; they considered themselves parts of a great team that eventually might make some sense out of what seemed to be not simple confusion, but often *organized confusion*.

I sent out some bulletins on the Bender affair to key people, asking their opinions. I received a great many replies.

One correspondent wondered if the government was secretly building a rocket ship, or artificial satellite. Had Bender found out about the project, planned to publish the information? Maybe he had submitted the information for publication, and was visited because security was involved. After all, such a project would represent a vital defense secret.

That could be the reason for the visit, the correspondent conjectured. What Bender was doing on saucers might not have been important, but if the mystery could have been switched from the actual thing to saucers, everyone would have been thrown off the track. The correspondent wondered if Bender were not cooperating thus with the government.

I had asked readers to use their imaginations freely, for in that process they might accidentally hit upon the real thing, which, as Bender had put it, was indeed fantastic.

One person took me at my word.

Could the saucers, he asked, have already landed, and have infiltrated even the government, either secretly or by force? Bender may have found out about this and written an article. The three men could then have confirmed his theory. Would not the fact that he had been face to face with extraterrestrials cause almost anyone to turn white and be sick for three days?

Another correspondent thought the Sun might be turning into a super nova, not an uncommon occurrence in the lifetimes of stars—and our Sun is a star. Although the government had known about it from confidential astronomical reports, they feared such a revelation would drive the citizenry into panic. A confirmation of this theory would, too, have made Bender ill.

Maybe there was nothing sinister at all in the closing of the IFSB, another correspondent suggested.

The government had suddenly become aware of the IFSB through a few concurrent happenings. The police in Jersey City had found the report which looked suspicious to them, and this information, together with the Clarksburg FBI agent's report about me, reached Washington about the same time.

Next one speculated that the government, at that time, was confused about the saucer mystery, having only some of the answers. They investigated the IFSB, learned Bender was too close to some of the answers they had. The government, wishing to prevent a civilian organization from knowing too much, sent agents of some kind to frighten Bender deliberately and put him on the wrong track. By telling him a horrifying story, probably fabricated, they were able to shut him up without ordering him outright to do so.

Seeing the IFSB letterheads alone would impress an outsider perhaps far too greatly. Perhaps this was the solution to the mystery in Bridgeport.

Coral E. Lorenzen, head of the Aerial Phenomena Research Organization, a similar, though smaller saucer investigative organization, threw up a trial balloon in her November 15, 1953 issue of *The Apro Bulletin.*

She believed a pulp magazine publisher had been secretly backing the IFSB. When the backer suddenly withdrew, Bender had no funds with which to run the organization, cooked up the fantastic story in order to get out from under the thing.

But to me this theory was even more fantastic than the saucers themselves might be.

Being in amateur publishing myself, I knew the membership fee Bender charged was enough to carry on the main expense of the IFSB, that of publishing the quarterly issues of *Space Review,* a small and relatively inexpensive publication. All work was volunteered; there were no salaries. And when Bender bowed out he made sure that refunds were made promptly to all members requesting them; to others he continued the publication in non-saucer format long enough to fulfill all subscriptions.

I would like to quell forever rumors that Bender used his organization for gain in any way, and that the closing was motivated by lack of funds.

A writer, whom many of you have read, but who asked me to preserve his anonymity, tried to resolve the mystery through psychological channels. In his research, he said, he had run across instances where unfortunate people had witnessed paranormal manifestations they could never bring themselves to discuss. One photographer had gone insane after developing a negative on which the image of a ghost appeared. But usually these people had simply refused to talk. Had Bender invented the three men to avoid talking about an experience that had been too terrible for words?

That the men wore dark clothing was perhaps the most puzzling aspect to most researchers who tried to evolve some theory to explain the IFSB closure.

Government agents, particularly if they wish their activities to be secret, do not dress conspicuously. A "secret agent" would find his secrecy falling from about him if he deliberately dressed to look like the popular conception of a "secret agent."

Bender himself later stated the visitors were not from the FBI, though on one occasion he did say they were "from another branch."

The odd clothing led Doreen A. Wilkinson, an investigator in New Zealand, to speculate that the black suits could have been clerical garb.

"If the saucer story is as we think, then it would have an adverse effect upon Biblical teachings. Naturally the church would not wish to see its teachings proved wrong. Maybe Bender went along with church dignitaries who called on him, to prevent people's ideas of religion from being shattered suddenly before their minds could be properly prepared."

The theory sounded unlikely, but nevertheless interesting. I have never discussed religion with Bender beyond generality and do not know to what faith, if any, he subscribes.

C. E. Hoover, of Pennsylvania, asked, "Would it be too fantastic to consider that the saucer people may have contacted Washington and other governments, requesting that reports and rumors of their actuality and purpose be kept at a minimum until a favorable time? By 'favorable' I mean a time and place best suited for open meeting. Somehow, I have the feeling that

President Eisenhower knows the utter futility of trying to preserve the peace of the world by stockpiling lethal weapons; I notice something of this in his recent speeches. Does old Army man Ike have definite knowledge of why the saucers are here?"

Bender himself answered Hoover's latter query in a subsequent interview with me. Not even the President had been told the secret of the saucers at that time, he said.

The oddness of the three mens' actions impressed one man whom I consulted. After going over the evidence I presented he formed the following conclusion:

"In my work as an engineer I have frequently worked on classified projects, and, as a result, have come in contact with not only the FBI, but the intelligence branches of the various armed services.

"The actions he reports are decidedly not typical of *any* of them. They simply do not work in that manner. As a matter of fact, the FBI never has done much on the saucer subject, and is less likely to be doing anything at the present time, because they are tied down by investigations into Communist activities. As for intelligence men, they seldom answer questions, or volunteer opinions, and certainly wouldn't issue any warnings. The fact is, most of them are *afraid* to express any opinions of their own—too much chance of being called on the carpet for talking out of turn.

"In any of the armed services it's not safe to even say that it is raining, unless the statement has been cleared by proper authority. As for saucers and the top brass, such a state of confusion exists there they can't form a policy on any phase of the subject."

One thing was becoming evident: if the three men did represent the government, the saucer situation must be growing into a problem of alarming size, else they would not be stepping out of character.

A communication from Paul Rear, one of my California informants, seemed to make sense.

Before Bender's "shush up" Rear received a letter from him, suggesting they collaborate on writing a book. With what Rear knew, added to Bender's knowledge, the latter was sure they could come up with something really startling.

But Rear didn't tell me what it was he knew that had excited Bender.

I got him on the phone.

"Let me have it, Paul. What is it you know that got Bender excited?"

"I'm sorry, but I can't discuss it over the phone," Rear said, "but there would be no harm done, I believe, in writing you something about it. I have no proof of the thing, and, if true, it might involve security."

"Can't you give me an inkling?" I protested, unable to wait.

"Basically it's about a secret meeting at the Hotel Statler in New York. I got wind of it through a friend of mine. Better let me write it to you, Gray."

It looked as if I'd have to wait.

The only thing Rear could think of that amazed Bender, he wrote, was his illustration of the fantastic changes that are to come to the Earth because of a new source of energy Rear believed we possessed. This new form of energy would do away with, for example, the automobile engine as we know it, revamp all ideas of electrical energy, kill the gas, oil and coal industries. All conventional fuels would be relegated to a past age.

It was *how* to make the changeover to the new kind of

power without causing a world economic collapse that had the government worried.

Rear had confirmation by sources who received letters from Washington. They were engineers and heads of large industrial concerns who were invited to the Statler under rigid security.

The subject for the meeting was veiled under the official designation, "Aircraft Engine Power," though Rear had an inkling that it was to be far more interesting than a mere discussion of new jet engines.

The discussions were to center around utilization of neutronic energy of a highly advanced nature, and it was hinted the secret had been learned from taking apart an interplanetary saucer.

Rear believed Bender had also received a similar invitation, through his membership in the American Rocket Society. He believed Bender had been amazed to learn he had similar knowledge.

During all this time Dom Lucchesi went on worrying about a possible link between the Bender Mystery and the Shaver Mystery. In New York one day, I was walking with Dom along 43rd Street.

"When I mentioned Shaver, why did he turn pale," Dom asked over and over, half addressing me, half talking to himself.

"If what Shaver says is true," I said, "why hasn't somebody found the caves and broken the story in the press? Why hasn't someone captured a dero and put him in a cage?" I figured that this line would put my friend off on one of his tangents, as usual.

It did.

"You remember what Shaver said. It's the world's best-kept secret. Better kept by far than the A-bomb secret."

He would prove it to me. Right there on 43rd Street.

Dom is daring. He walked up to a well-dressed, intelligent-looking fellow and asked directions. Then he said to the unsuspecting test subject:

"Sir, do you know that beneath this very street, hundreds o maybe even thousands of feet down, there lives a race of peopl who are called dero?"

"Have you gone nuts!" the man replied, and hastily seeking exit between us, muttered, as he left, "You have the oddest scheme for panhandling I've ever run across."

* * * * *

"Men in dark suits," Bender had said.

I kept conning over to myself, "Black suits . . . black suits. . . ."

No, it wasn't the reference Mary Hyde, a researcher of Alexandria, Virginia, suggested. She remembered having read about some people who wore dark suits. They were sylphs, spirits of some kind, who could take the form of men when they desired to. But Mary probably was pulling my leg. That was like her. I was glad that at least a *few* investigators could still retain their senses of humor.

"Black suits . . . black suits. . . ."

And Maury Island!

That was it! A fellow in a black suit had threatened a witness to a spectacular sighting. Who was the man who told the story to Kenneth Arnold? "Doyle," "Derhl," or something like that.

I pulled out my file on the Maury Island case.

Most of the notes were taken from a manuscript privately published by Ray Palmer, titled *The Coming of the Saucers,*

147

now out of print. I remembered saying to someone it was the most fascinating saucer book I had ever read.

It told how Palmer sent Arnold, famous for first coining the term, "flying saucer," to Tacoma, Washington, to check up on a story Harold A. Dahl and Fred L. Crissman, two harbor patrolmen, had told.

Dahl was patrolling in his boat at Maury Island, near Tacoma, when he and his crew saw six huge doughnut-shaped objects in the sky. They appeared to be about 100 feet in diameter, of bright metallic coloring. Portholes were spaced around the outside of the things, and inside the "holes" of the "doughnuts" were dark, circular, continuous windows. Five of the objects were circling around the sixth, which seemed to be in mechanical trouble.

Suddenly they heard a muffled explosion, and the sixth object discharged a great quantity of metallic residue, something like lava rock, which fell all around them. Some of the fragments hit the boat, causing considerable damage. One of them killed a dog and another injured Dahl's son. The five remaining objects flew off.

Dahl, along with Crissman, to whom he later related the occurrence, collected some of the slag-like residue as well as some mysterious white metal that accompanied the fall.

The famous "Project Saucer" report of April 27, 1949, a resume of investigations by the Air Materiel Command at Wright Field, contained an account of the Maury Island affair.

Arnold summoned two officers of Army A-2 Intelligence to assist him in investigating the claims of Dahl and Crissman. The two investigators, Captain William L. Davidson, and Lieutenant Frank M. Brown, arrived and questioned the parties involved, accepting a package of the fragments from Crissman. Brown

148

was in reality a counter-espionage agent, according to Arnold. Even though he assumed the title of Second Lieutenant as an A-2 Intelligence officer, in reality he had a much higher rating, receiving orders direct from Mitchell Field, New York, and had the authority to assume the rank of a five-star general if the need arose.

But tragedy struck the two officers. Their plane crashed while leaving Tacoma, under unusual circumstances. Both of them were killed. A mysterious telephone informant, who frequently called up Ted Morello, head of the Tacoma United Press office, was able to advise him of everything that was transpiring in Arnold's hotel room. The informant advised Morello the plane had been sabotaged.

Immediately after Arnold's investigation both Dahl and Crissman disappeared mysteriously, the latter shipped off to Alaska on an Army bomber, it was hinted by the telephone informant. "Project Saucer" concluded the Tacoma affair had been a hoax.

Maybe it was, I conceded, but that seemed to be the usual position taken by Air Force investigations.

But what struck me was Dahl's account of a visitor who called at his home the morning after the weird experience on Maury Island. The man, *who wore a black suit,* invited him to breakfast.

While they drove to a restaurant the visitor was reticent about relating what he wished to discuss. But as soon as they sat down to eat the man began telling Dahl everything that happened to him the day before, down to the most minute détail. Dahl was speechless. It seemed as if the man had actually been there with him, witnessing every action of the doughnut-shaped objects

As Dahl sat there, shaken and speechless, the visitor began to threaten him in a strange manner.

"What I have said is proof to you that I know a great deal more about this experience of yours than you will want to believe."

Dahl and Crissman had witnessed something they shouldn't have seen, just why, he didn't say. But he had some "sound advice" for them.

If Dahl loved his family and didn't want anything bad to happen he would not discuss the experience with anyone. Dahl related the happenings on the island to Arnold only after much persuasion.

At the time of the visit Dahl told Arnold he thought the man was a crackpot, had gone ahead and told the story. Since that time, however, some peculiar things had happened, and he feared he should have taken the stranger's advice.

This would not necessarily mean that the same man, in the company of two others, had visited Bender. After all, a great many people wore black suits. But something in the manner of the three men's dress had impressed Bender deeply. I knew that, for he seemed to ascribe importance to the dark clothing.

But the more I thought about the IFSB closure, and the more theories I considered, the farther from an explanation I wandered. I soon realized that the mere casting about for wild theories explaining the fold-up could provide no real answer.

The next time I was in New York I decided to go to Bridgeport and talk to Bender personally, and I took along Roberts and Lucchesi.

X

Australia

The man is a friend of yours.

But he knows something you'd almost give your right arm to know yourself. He claims to know what the saucers really are.

He has cracked the sphinxlike riddle, but the keepers of the secret have nevertheless exacted an awful penalty. He is on his honor as an American citizen, he says, not to reveal the answer to the cosmic conundrum.

When Bender met us at the door I knew I wouldn't have the courage to pump him and try to wrest the secret from him. I put myself in his shoes. If he did tell us something significant, would we, after all, respect him for doing so, if he were indeed under security? Surely the government, more than we saucer investigators, was in a position to know what was best for the country.

I decided we would make it a personal visit, would not take advantage of the man's warm hospitality. I was somewhat ashamed of how I had influenced my other two friends to play the question-and-answer game you have read about in a previous chapter.

But it seemed that Al himself wanted to discuss his experiences further, though none of us pushed the issue.

"Try to put yourself into my shoes," I said to him. "If you were I, and had been visited by the three men, do you think I would have kept my mouth shut as you have done?"

"No. Knowing you, I don't believe you would have."

"In your own personal opinion, Al, can you tell me this: do you think you should have been told you couldn't release the information that you have?"

"No, I don't, Gray."

I began to realize the peculiar position into which Bender had been shoved. Here was a man who had left no stone unturned in getting saucer information before the world. Suddenly he found himself in a position where he could say practically nothing. I knew he was dying to tell us, but could not.

But it did seem a change had come over Bender. His former enthusiasm about saucer research and his organization had evaporated. He shied away from the word, "saucer," as if it held some unpleasant connotation.

Another visitor, he did tell us, had been to his house since his meeting with the three men. This follow-up visitor gave him a broader picture of the situation and led him to feel somewhat better about the entire matter. But again, he could give us little information about the nature of the visitor or what he discussed.

He expected to be absent frequently since it was necessary that he go to Washington occasionally, though he did not elaborate with reasons.

We passed most of the day talking of other mutual interests, though when we were preparing to leave one additional surprise awaited me.

"Before you go, I'd like you to read this letter from Jarrold," Bender said, handing me a communication written on the letterhead of The Australian Flying Saucer Bureau.

Edgar R. Jarrold had formed the Australian organization about the same time the IFSB had been launched. The two organizations exchanged information.

Jarrold had received a visit, too, I learned with amazement, though Bender said he didn't know if it involved a similar kind of emissary.

Jarrold's visitor, too, had arrived unexpectedly, had announced he had certain information on saucers to give the investigator.

He exacted Jarrold's word of honor, however, not to reveal anything that subsequently passed between them, without first receiving permission.

In order to obtain the information Jarrold had no recourse other than to agree to silence. It was particularly emphasized he was to tell *nobody*—not even his wife.

Some of the things the visitor told him were to be written down in his presence, but he would not permit other things to be recorded in writing.

What the visitor told Jarrold amazed him "beyond description," though he said he wasn't frightened. He did add he could

153

not guarantee others might not have been terrified, and "scared out of their wits by what passed."

Jarrold was also advised the title, The Australian Flying Saucer Bureau, was not a very good one. The visitor suggested an alternate, Interplanetary Ships Sighting Bureau.

After we were in Roberts' car, driving back to his and Lucchesi's homes, none of us said anything for a long time. We were all thinking similarly.

Finally I broke the silence.

"Well, what did you think of it?"

Lucchesi knew I meant the letter from Jarrold.

"It looks like a pattern all right. We may be next."

"I wonder if Jarrold is out of action," Roberts interjected.

"It doesn't look that way. Jarrold's letter says nothing about being 'shushed up.'"

Jarrold's letter sounded as if he had heard about the strange goings-on in Bridgeport. Perhaps Bender may have told him more than he told us.

"It looks as if the three of us will have to form some sort of organization to crack this thing," I said. "Are you two with me?"

They said they'd stick it out with me until the last gun was fired.

Or, as Lucchesi, always able, it seemed, to preserve his sense of humor, said, "To the last cup and saucer."

"To the last cup and saucer!" Roberts and I repeated, almost in unison.

It seemed the next thing to do was to get in touch with Jarrold and ask him point-blank about the letter, advising him I had seen it. I would also write to Harold Fulton, head of the Civilian Saucer Investigation of New Zealand, who, as I knew, was personally acquainted with Jarrold and might throw more light onto the subject—if he, himself, had not already been approached.

What I was to learn from Australia and New Zealand was to thicken the plot of what seemed to be too fantastic to be real, and surely must be a story we were only acting out, not too well, I was afraid.

The letter I received from Jarrold didn't sound like fiction. He confirmed writing the letter to Bender, filled me in on more details. It was a long communication, and I can quote only a part of it. Jarrold first answered some questions I had put to him, one by one:

"1. Regarding the visit mentioned in my letter to Al Bender, not one, but four such visits were received at headquarters here —on December 3, 5, 7 and 12 respectively.

"2. The material higher on this page already contains our official statement that no talks regarding saucers have as yet ensued with any government department or representatives on an official basis.

"3. The visitor I received *did not* tell me to close down the AFSB. In fact, in reply to a natural query as to whether this was the purpose of his visit, he appeared surprised and taken aback, and denied the suggestion.

"4. Each visit was unofficial and private, the first being quite unexpected. The visitor announced that he had some amazing but highly important information regarding flying saucers to convey to me—but that before doing so it was imperative that I give my word of honor not to reveal *anything of what occurred*, until permission to do so was received.

"To this I objected, on the ground that my silence would be

unfair to AFSB members and others, to which the visitor remained adamant, persisting that unless this condition was observed he could tell me nothing.

"Finally, as the only means of obtaining the information from him, I agreed. In discussions which lasted for three hours the visitor then conveyed information which amazed me beyond description. At one stage of the conversation I was asked to reply to a certain question 'without thinking or hesitating in the slightest degree for even a moment.' This question was, 'What do you think would happen to extraterrestrial visitors immediately if a saucer landed close to Sydney, or any other large city?'

"Candidly and honestly, I replied at once, 'The occupants would be murdered out of hand—although ironically probably the greatest care would be taken to ensure the capture of their space vehicle undamaged.'

"This dangerous ignorance and hostility, the visitor assured me, is the main reason preventing extraterrestrial beings from landing openly at present. The visitor announced that it was known that they could use 'horrifying destructive forces' but gave his opinion that the visitors would not use these forces, since to do so would prove disastrous to further contact, and they apparently seek only friendly contact.

"5. This and other information the visitor disclosed revealed the most fantastic situation it seems possible to conceive by normal standards.

"6. The information did not frighten me, although I would not guarantee that others would not have been terrified. I was amazed, but too busy listening to what the visitor said to consider any other feelings.

"7. The visitor in my presence on December 3 produced

156

evidence attesting to his position and qualifications. I could see no useful purpose being served by his revealing such astounding information if it was untrue; it was given candidly and seriously, and no effort was made to deny either the existence of 'saucers' or intelligent occupants. The purpose in his visiting me, the visitor remarked, was to place at my disposal certain information and advice considered essential at this stage. It was repeatedly stressed that the reasons for my selection as the recipient were my 'sincerity and lack of hostility.' "

Although Jarrold's visitor seemed to act differently than did the three men visiting Bender (if the latter had given us the correct information), there was a similarity between the two events.

As I tried to analyze the similarity I suddenly remembered Jarrold's November issue.

Why had I not been impressed before!

Theatre problems were taking more and more of my time. I had been able only to scan much of the saucer information reaching me, and in the rush, I had tossed aside the November, 1953, issue of *The Australian Flying Saucer Magazine,* without realizing the editorial said some mighty spooky things.

"In early September sensational happenings occurred at the headquarters of the International Flying Saucer Bureau, in Bridgeport, Connecticut. The first intimation the Australian Bureau received of anything unusual came like a bombshell during AFSB, CSI (New Zealand), and IFSB discussions regarding proposed joint investigations into a certain United States theory re saucers supplied by Mr. Bender."

Here was another clue! Whatever Bender found out, and whatever was responsible for closing him down, likely had something to do with this "joint investigation" Jarrold mentioned!

But just what was the "joint investigation" *investigating?* What ever its nature it surely was confidential, for it had not been mentioned in Jarrold's publication, beyond the single reference, nor had Harold H. Fulton, head of Civilian Saucer Investigation of New Zealand, so much as breathed about it in voluminous correspondence directed to me.

I must get to Fulton immediately, now that it appeared Jarrold could no longer talk freely.

Then I noted other peculiar paragraphs in Jarrold's editorial:

"Analysing the events leading up to the fate of IFSB, and the last issue of *Space Review,* one immensely important conclusion can be drawn—and that is, if the facts are exactly as they appear to be, the surfeit of theories regarding actual flying saucer origin has been drastically reduced to not more than two. One of these is that saucers originate from Mars—with all that that momentous fact conveys and implies."

And read the next paragraph carefully:

"The other theory involves a staggering event which, unfortunately, for very vital reasons, cannot be revealed—or even discussed theoretically—by the President of the AFSB until specific additional data (not currently in the possession of the AFSB) has either been established or rejected with positive certainty. All that can be conveyed here is that the particular information emphasises the *cause* of flying saucers rather than their *origin.*"

Whatever Jarrold was saying, it was a mouthful.

Things were adding up—fast!

There *was* a parallel between Jarrold's visitor and Bender's three men! Jarrold had arrived at some kind of hypothesis regarding the saucer mystery, one he felt must almost definitely be IT. He had arrived at this hypothesis *before* being visited, just as Bender had done. For Jarrold's first visit occurred on December 3, after the magazine had come out.

And whatever Jarrold had decided about saucers, it didn't sound at all pleasant, though the writer did not specifically say it involved something catastrophic.

If Jarrold could release what he had found out or evolved through theory, surely he would have added this information in his letter to me about the visitor.

I knew the only thing to do was to get to Fulton in New Zealand. If only *they* had not reached him first. I explained my position in the matter, informed him fully of what was happening in Bridgeport, and gave him the gist of Jarrold's unusual communication.

"I haven't heard from Jarrold lately," Fulton replied. "It looks like he's really knocked out."

Fulton said he thought it was about time he opened his confidential files for my use.

"If I don't now, it looks as if I might not be *able* to do so later."

A few days later the Fulton files were in my hands.

XI

Antarctica

This may have nothing to do with flying saucers.

It is a tale of abominable stenches and eldritch bangings in the night.

It is a true story.

You are Harold H. Fulton.

It is with reluctance that you relate these personal experiences from your confidential file. After all, they may have nothing at all to do with Bender and his troubles, but you feel the story will not be complete without them.

It is late afternoon, July 21, 1953, and you are busy taking care of CSI administrative details. You are all wool gathered, and your Siamese cat persists in making that odd growling noise, a sound that seems to come from somewhere deep within her insides. You investigate. She is on the window sill, deeply disturbed by something outside the window.

You look. There is nothing there.

You say, "Look, silly," pick her up and are going to hold her outside the window. The cat becomes terrified, and you realize she will attack you if you persist.

As far as you know, there is nothing strange or terrifying outside the window. Though, come to think of it, you did detect a strange odor.

You forget about it.

When Fulton left the house on the morning of August 18, the matter of the cat and the open window and the stench came back to him. For here again was that very same odor, though now stronger and even more unpleasant. When he returned that evening his wife met him with an odd story.

She had noticed an unusual odor at the back door. The cat wanted out, but when she opened the door it recoiled rapidly, hissed and spat, leaped into the air and retreated into the bedroom.

A few nights later Mr. and Mrs. Fulton were awakened in the early hours of the morning by a loud and violent pounding on the outside of the house. The noise stopped abruptly, then began again.

Mrs. Fulton was the first to become completely aroused from slumber, and she sat up in bed. She saw what appeared to be an orange-pink glow near the door, screamed and hid under the bedclothes.

Fulton jumped from bed, went through the house, looked on the outside.

Nothing!

This occurred before Bender was so finally silenced, while he was still corresponding enthusiastically with the "down under" saucer groups. The next day Fulton had a letter from him. It was a routine communication, except for one offhand query: Bender supposed Fulton had heard about Jarrold's experience with the unusual odor!

Fulton almost jumped out of his desk chair.

So Jarrold ran into the odor, too! He lost little time communicating with the head of the Australian group. What Jarrold told him made him feel he had attached too little importance to the odd sequence of events.

Just as the August issue of Jarrold's publication was going to press, a series of puzzling, but apparently related incidents had occurred at the AFSB headquarters in Fairfield. Jarrold could find no meaning or purpose behind the happenings, merely related them for Fulton's reference and comparison.

On July 21, about 2:45 A.M., Jarrold was awakened by a pounding noise outside his house. He ran outside in the direction from which the noise apparently originated, but found no explanation. Instead he encountered a strange odor, suggestive of burning plastic, or that was the only way he could describe it, he said.

He called the Liverpool Police, who investigated promptly but drew a blank, advising Jarrold someone must be pulling a hoax or a publicity stunt. The AFSB director was dissatisfied with that explanation, investigated further, and found neighbors who had also heard the pounding, though they had not smelled the odor.

The event did not disturb Jarrold until the next night when he couldn't stop thinking about it after going to bed. Maybe the backbreaking work of administering the Bureau was getting him down, and he was "hearing things." Maybe he should take it a little easier.

He dozed fitfully, wakening often. Far too many automobiles were passing for that time of night. He arose to make a pot of tea, looked outside as he heard another car pass the house.

That was odd! The car had its lights off. Particularly odd for this section of town—Jarrold had persistently goaded the city about installing better illumination in his neighborhood. The same car passed again. And again! It seemed as if someone were looking his place over. It was too dark to see who was inside, but as his eyes got used to the blackness he made out two shadowy shapes huddled in the front seat of the black limousine. The next time the car came it parked on the other side of the street, a quarter of a block past his house.

Jarrold didn't call the police; they probably wouldn't come anyway, thinking he was "just imagining things," as one of them had summed up the story about the poundings and the odor. That was 3:00 A.M. The car remained parked until 6:30 P.M.

The next morning Jarrold inquired if anyone else had seen the car. One of his friends had! This individual, whom Jarrold would not name, saw one of the riders clearly when the car stopped and a man leaned out to ask what time it was. The man was a known criminal, police told him after he described the suspicious character to them.

Jarrold suggested no publicity should be accorded the happenings, since it might be of dubious benefit to saucer research and attach a possibly unnecessary mystery angle to the work. The two ascribed importance to the occurrences only because of the coincidence of time and involvement of two saucer researchers.

As Fulton read an issue of *The Apro Bulletin* some time later he reviewed the happenings in his own home, particularly his cat's strange terror.

He was reading about a woman sitting up keeping watch over her sick daughter late at night. Her husband was working.

She was reading, uninterrupted by the music from the radio except when infrequent commercials intruded.

The radio suddenly set up a terrific noise. Uncomfortably loud static was blotting out the program. When she switched the dial she found the static was all over the band.

When she snapped the radio off to stop the noise, it was replaced by another sound, sometimes coming from the back yard, often seeming to surround her. It was a kind of thrumming sound, a kind of deep musical note enveloped in vibrating harmonics. It was the weirdest sound she had ever heard.

Her dog, usually a quiet animal, now was growling with bared fangs. There must be a burglar in the house, she thought, not yet attaching any significance to the thrumming sound. Then she looked out the window into the back yard. It was lighted up like daylight! She decided the light must be coming from directly above, since the shrubbery threw very little shadow. Later she wondered why she had been so bravely analytical, as she recalled how she started to go outside to look into the matter but was stopped by the dog, backed up against the door, snarling. She reached for the doorknob, and the dog barked fiercely and crouched as if he would leap at her.

Then she realized the dog must be terrified at what was outside, was preventing her from exposing herself to the danger. If the dog was frightened, why shouldn't she be? This realization struck great terror into her, and she went almost limp. She staggered back into her chair, and the dog ran to her, huddled beside her, shivering and growling.

Abruptly the noise terminated. She crept to the window; it was again dark outside. The dog began to romp around the room, playing with a rubber bone. She turned the radio on again and it played normally.

But I'm afraid we're going far afield of Bender. Of the three men and Jarrold's strange visitor.

And "Project X."

"From Mr. Bender's ominous appearing message, it would seem wise to suspend further investigations into Project X until after we have both received the Oct. 15 *Space Review*," Jarrold wrote Fulton. This was before Jarrold arrived at his own terrifying hypothesis.

"Project X."

That was a new one!

Why had not Jarrold or Fulton mentioned it in their correspondence with me?

Maybe it was something so fantastic they feared I would laugh at them. But the entire saucer field was becoming, day by day, so fantastic that now few people were laughing.

Though Fulton had opened his files on Bender to me, he had divulged nothing about "Project X."

Could it be the Antarctic Theory, mentioned by Bender in his letter to Jarrold dated September 14? In this he had said, "We would like to refrain from comment on that until after our October 15 issue is published."

While I was talking with Bender he visibly started when I mentioned the South Pole. And in Roberts' notes on his and

Lucchesi's interview with Bender there was a pertinent exchange: "Q: Does this have anything to do with the South Pole?" —"A: I can't answer that." What, if anything, linked the South Pole with the three men in black and the solution to the saucer mystery?

I had never connected Antarctica with saucers, though I did recall that Admiral Richard E. Byrd had seen some mighty queer things during his expeditions to Little America.

What about the man of Long Island, New York, who did not seem to be interested in saucers but was shouting his head off about a catastrophic event which would take place if someone didn't listen to him? Both Bender and Jarrold gave the impression that they feared an impending catastrophe. Was it the same one? Maybe the Long Islander was right, and somehow the saucers *were* connected. Maybe they were here to warn us or to evacuate the planet.

Hugh A. Brown is surely no crackpot. He holds a degree in electrical engineering from Columbia University, operates a prosperous business at Douglaston, Long Island. For the past 40 years he has been slowly and carefully gathering data on what he terms "mankind's glistening executioner"—the ice cap at the South Pole.

Brown screams his head off trying to get someone to listen to him—and to do something about it. So far the public has refused to be frightened, but that is understandable: it is still an obscure theory and most of the people who have heard about it don't know enough about physics to understand everything Brown is talking about.

Brown almost wore out his knuckles beating on the doors of New York publishers, trying to get his hypothesis in print. But, perhaps unfortunately in many cases, publishers must necessarily be a practical lot. They must be able to *sell* books and can no longer afford to print volumes with the exclusive idea of educating the public.

One of them took two days to listen to Brown expound his theories. Finally he handed the bulky manuscript back to him.

"I understand what you are saying and I must say you have presented a good case, but . . ."

In trying to prove his alarming theory Brown had been quite technical.

"The people who can understand your book won't buy it. Recognized scientists could understand what you're saying, but they wouldn't believe you. They'd call you a crackpot. Throughout history no one with a genuinely brand-new idea has been listened to, especially when that idea tears down beliefs the reigning intellectuals have established as supreme. Even if they did find your data logical they'd let the world go ahead and do the flip-flop before they'd admit you were right."

Allowing the disaster to occur, the publishers said with a wry smile, would be less trouble to them than rewriting all the textbooks.

"To obtain action on the kind of project you propose would involve getting the public behind you. If they believed you they could force Congress to take action. But unfortunately the public won't buy your book. If they did they wouldn't know what you were talking about."

"They *must* be told!" Brown, agitated with the urgency of the situation, almost shouted.

"Take it home and rewrite it in non-technical terms and I'll buy it," the publisher promised.

But without the technical proofs Brown didn't see how it could be done and instead he busily sends out pamphlets, calling the crisis to the attention of anyone who will listen, warning of great immediate danger hanging over everyone's head like the legendary Sword of Damocles.

There probably never really was a Damocles but the story is entertaining, if somewhat moralistic. He was a Syracusan who was being entertained at the court of Dionysius.

During his stay at the court Damocles was greatly impressed by the splendor and power he saw there, and constantly glorified his host. As an object lesson to his guest Dionysius gave a great banquet in his honor.

Amid the revelry Damocles happened to look toward the ceiling, took a deep breath and probably dropped his wineglass. For there, hanging over his head, was a huge sword, suspended by a single hair. At any moment the hair might snap, allowing death to descend upon him.

Dionysius told the frightened guest the sword was suspended there as an object lesson, to demonstrate that wealth and power are fraught with impermanence, worry, unhappiness and tragedy.

But Brown's book was not written as an object lesson. It was a thesis, couched in cold scientific terms, crying out that the human race, and perhaps all life on the Earth, faces immediate extinction.

For the ice at the South Pole, if it continues to accumulate unchecked, will one day cause the Earth to shiver, careen over on its side, tipping over like a giant overloaded canoe. The ensuing floods and other great natural upheavals will spell doom for humans everywhere, excepting a few who might be in the right places on the Earth at the right time.

The Earth, Brown explains to orthodox scientists who look down their noses at him, does not spin on center, and the same orthodox scientists, who have never made any great effort to disprove his theories, admit the globe wobbles slightly in its rotation.

Because the great ice cap is consequently not in the center of the axis, it tends to cause a greater wobble, the off-center rotation creating an eccentric centrifugal force. This eccentric motion could flip the Earth over and create a new axis of rotation, in which the poles would change places with points on the equatorial belt. But the effect of this eccentric motion fortunately is checked by the equatorial bulge, which also creates a centrifugal force through the power of the spinning globe. This acts like a huge gyroscope, preventing the Earth from careening. Sooner or later, however, as the ice cap gains more mass, the gyroscopic action of the bulge will no longer be able to prevent catastrophe.

The ice now covers 6,000,000 square miles, about double the area of the United States, and is piled up more than two miles thick at the center. If spread out it would make a layer about 120 feet deep over the entire globe.

The ponderous size of the ice cap is not Brown's primary concern. The fact that it is growing at the rate of five trillion tons each year is what keeps the engineer turning over and over in his bed at night. Sooner or later, maybe even tomorrow or next week, or even the next minute, the zero hour will surely arrive, unless drastic steps are taken.

The cataclysm will be nothing new, declares Brown, and he proceeds to cite plenty of proofs drawn from the long history of the planet. Again and again, these proofs indicate, Earth's axis has shifted and polar wastes have become tropical belts. In previous cycles, he believes, it has taken approximately 6,000 years for the polar ice caps to build up to a thickness too massive to be counteracted by the equatorial bulge. But in his estimate the present cycle has been in progress for almost 8,000 years.

If his basic thesis is correct, the onset of the next world flood appears to be distressingly overdue.

Fossils of certain plants and animals have been found in arctic regions, Brown points out; this proves that in the dim past the now frigid regions must have been tropical ones. Geologists agree that the Alps, Andes, Himalayas and other great mountain systems were once under the sea, and admit, with almost the same breath, that the topography of the ocean floor is not unlike that of land. It would seem to Brown that once upon a time, maybe many times over, land and sea areas rapidly traded places.

In comparison with man's knowledge, or pseudo knowledge, of land areas, little is known about the sea. Marine expeditions have puzzled over the depth of the sediment on the ocean floor, finding it not as deep as it should be, considering the supposed age of the oceans. Similar sediments on land areas, which the ocean once covered, are much deeper! The oceans surely covered the land during longer periods than mankind has supposed!

Rocks are uninteresting to most people, but geologists who pry among them are able to find them a great source of excitement. Not long ago the geologists ran into a problem that had them babbling with confusion and heated argument, and almost hurling their rocks at one another. They found the magnetism of certain rocks was not right; the alignment of the magnetic lines of force was exactly backward to what it should be, as if the magnetic poles of the Earth had once occupied a completely different area than they do today!

There was only one answer to this puzzler, but one the geologists were loath to accept: at the time the rocks cooled the magnetic poles of the Earth were completely in reverse of their present location!

Lava rock receives its magnetic property while cooling. The magnetic orientation is taken on from the Earth when the rock cools to a certain temperature, after which, in cooling further, it retains that same orientation. If the magnetic poles of the Earth should change after the cooling, the rock would not be affected, unless it happened to be still in molten state after the poles were so reversed.

When the Earth flips over the action will be sudden, Brown declares, and as evidence he points to an enigma that has long puzzled its investigators. The frozen bodies of mammoths, extinct since caveman days, were found early in this century in the tundras of northern Siberia. The bodies were well preserved, and sledge dogs ate of the flesh without harm. Upon death the animals were chewing on mouthfuls of a food also found in their viscera, offering proof of two almost unbelievable things. The mammoths lived among abundant vegetation, in an area where there has been no adequate vegetation for more than 7,000 years. But the biggest puzzler was the nature of their deaths and the preservation of their bodies. Some of them had broken bones, indicating violent contusions just prior to death, others appeared to have frozen to death while standing on their feet. Whatever catastrophe had maimed some of the animals was also accompanied by a sudden cold, for their bodies looked as if they had been thrown suddenly into a huge food freezer. Under ordinary circumstances their bodies would have decomposed before they could have been preserved by freezing.

The evidence points, Brown believes, to a sudden reversal of positions btween tropical and polar regions, accompanied by the great upheavals such a sudden change would involve.

Some students of prehistoric animal life have brought up a matter which further backs up Brown's contention that Earth's history has been punctuated with sudden and violent paroxysms. There is a contradiction, they say, in the apparent fact that the mammoth should have become extinct because of failure to adapt, for the mammoth was a better-developed animal than the elephant. Were all extinct species of prehistoric animal life wiped out because of their inability to adapt to environmental changes? Or were many species destroyed by sudden and violent cataclysms? Fossils are not being formed today, these students remind us, and they point to cataclysm as a condition for forming and preserving them.

One of the biggest questions orthodox scientists have left unanswered, states Brown, is *how* dinosaur tracks and even raindrop splashes could have been preserved in rock as fossils. Nowadays take your dog for a walk and let him step in mud. His tracks will remain, but not for long. The mud will ooze back to fill in the tracks and the next rain will fully obliterate them. Surely they will not endure for the thousands of years necessary for the mud to turn to stone, leaving the tracks permanently imprinted. Let your dog walk on a freshly laid concrete walk, however, and his footprints will be left for posterity and for future historians to examine, provided they are interested in dog tracks at that time. Since the wrath of the city maintenance department may greatly overbalance the joy of such a contribution to future geological museums, this instance is used as an example only, to point out that there seems to be only one answer, which bears out Brown's theory of the careening globe. Fossilized tracks must have frozen suddenly, quickly after they were made by animals, by some sudden and tremendous change of climate. The frozen mud thus in time became stone, with the tracks still imprinted on it.

A mountain of evidence thus points to a flip of the globe which abruptly left the ice caps of the poles melting in tropical heat, while what once were equatorial areas froze over almost instantly as they became the new Arctic regions.

Little or no life will survive the catastrophe if mankind lets it happen, asserts Brown. The flip will be sudden, and the atmosphere, which normally moves along with the globe in its rotation, will not keep pace with the Earth as it careens. Winds of far greater than ordinary hurricane force will shriek across the land. The inertia of the water in the oceans will prevent its following the Earth, and the land areas will be inundated, as if water had been spilled on them from an unbelievably titanic dish.

The great play of energy involved will be partly dissipated as heat, causing rocks to melt and volcanoes to erupt. The weather will be chaotic until once again the Earth settles down to its new equilibrium. Then everything will be peaceful until the next great civilization is wiped out by another ice cap.

Some animal life and probably some vestiges of civilization survived in four locations at the time of the last great deluge. Brown believes these points were the former North and South Poles, now the Sudan Basin of Africa and the Samoan Island region in the Pacific Ocean, and two pivot areas, the Sumatra and Malaya region, and Peru and Ecuador in South America. In the event of a future repetition of the catastrophe, corresponding areas will be the safest locations, and probably life will survive there.

Normally ice breaks off at the South Pole in the form of icebergs, and an uneasy equilibrium is maintained. Lately, however, the ice has been forming faster than it has been breaking away. The United States Navy, states Brown, has ships in the region investigating his claims.

The swifter accumulation of ice is perhaps due to a part of space the Earth is now passing through, believes the engineer. He thinks cosmic ray bombardment, directed mainly at the "top" of the Earth, where the ice cap at the North Pole is melting, may have something to do with it. Perhaps as the Earth travels through different regions of space it runs into concentrations of cosmic rays, or meteoric dust, which affects temperatures on certain portions of the planet.

Whatever is responsible, the "glistening executioner" is growing monstrously in size and threatens to strike at any moment.

But what to do about it?

Most prognosticators of doom recommend that mankind repent, that humanity call upon spiritual entities of one kind or another to step in as saviors. Brown suggests a more materialistic and perhaps a more practical course.

Brown has a solution.

The only man-made force capable of making a consequential dent in the ice cap is the atomic or H-bomb, and Brown's voice now rises feebly, but with gathering strength as his hypothesis gets around, a voice crying that the bomb should be used. Not only bombs but money for research is needed, he declares.

Brown points out that the same catastrophe has repeated itself many times before, suggests the half-forgotten tales of our folklores may be vestigial evidences of real occurrences.

Is the story of Noah's flood the twisted narrative of what actually happened when the globe flipped over thousands of years ago, the racial memory of a few who escaped the terror and the madness? Are the legends of Atlantis and Lemuria, the traditions telling of their destruction by great natural forces, true stories, partly distorted chronicles of actual civilizations which occupied the Earth in another day, when another ice cap was growing?

The memory of a great deluge does not survive in Jewish history alone. Many legends and written records tell of similar catastrophes in the dim pasts of the Assyrians, Babylonians, Chaldeans. North and South American sources tell of a similar tradition. Greek mythology relates how Zeus allowed a great flood to wipe out the human race because of its iniquity. Instead of Noah and his family, it was one man and his wife, Deucalion and Pyrrha, who were saved, in an ark which came to rest on Mt. Parnassus, a corollary, perhaps, to Mt. Ararat, where Noah's ark purportedly touched dry land.

Trying to connect Antarctica with the flying saucers, I wondered if the disks, their occupants having detected the oncoming catastrophe from outer space, or wherever they live, might be coming here to check up. I wondered if such an expedition could be for cold academic study, or if perhaps its purpose was to find some way to prevent the Earth from careening.

I hoped it was the latter.

In thinking back over the legends of the last deluge I remembered a theme running through most of the accounts. Someone had built a boat, under divine inspiration, or had been taken aboard one, and so had survived the flood.

If the Earth should careen, as Brown predicts, and space people should rescue a few inhabitants of the human race, setting them back down on Earth again when the troubled days had passed, would not the descendants of these seeders of the

175

new Earth interpret the intervention as divine? Especially as the events became more and more garbled by the tellers of history?

Was it possible, I thought as I considered the problem, that many deities of great religions had been physical in origin and reality, and only thought of, by mankind, as gods?

I wondered.

Why had Bender, in Connecticut, and Jarrold, in Australia, been concerned with Antarctica? Was their interest connected somehow with Brown and his melancholy prophecy? Had they discovered that Brown was only partly right, had foretold doom properly but was wrong in how it was to come about?

XII

California

Bender had been evasive and close-mouthed about everything except his fear. Could I find some clues if I cast about for other prognostications of disaster? They were to be found widely, among people who had found time to draw partly aside from the mad race of living in order to consider and talk about such matters.

I couldn't neglect Meade Layne. He was on the level, all right, but I hoped some of his theories were fallacious. For his organization, the BSRA (Borderland Sciences Research Associates*), believed dire debacles were in the making. He also propounded an interesting new twist in saucer theories.

He believed the saucers were in "4-D"!

"Just as there is a spectrum of sound and color (ending in sounds we cannot hear and colors we cannot see)," Layne explains, "so there is also a spectrum of tangibility, ending in forms of matters which are too dense to be touched."

If you think Layne said a mouthful, wait until I tell you more about his theories, which I will try to break down into everyday language, as opposed to the somewhat technical verbiage in which they are ordinarily couched—for in Layne's association are a great many members with engineering and other scientific backgrounds.

His theories are so unusual you are not going to believe them offhand; to complicate matters some of his information comes from what the man on the street might term "the spirit world." And it helps matters none that Layne isn't able to take you into a secret laboratory and show you a "4-D" saucer.

I didn't want to believe his theory either, for it conflicted with my own saucer hypotheses. But like so many others who came to scoff and stayed to say, "Pray tell me more," I might as well come out and admit that regardless of how outlandish the whole thing sounds when you first run into it, the theories begin to make sense after you consider them for a while.

No wonder official publications refer to authors of contributions to BSRA literature by membership numbers. Many of the scientific minds who secretly contribute their findings to the organization do not wish colleagues to know they even belong to the group.

For the BSRA has been poking around in matters sci-

---

* 3524 Adams Ave., San Diego 16, Calif.

entists would say were none of its business for a great many years. It is "an association of persons interested in 'borderland' facts and happenings . . . facts and events which orthodox or official science cannot or will not investigate." In a day when orthodox science is on the frontier of atomics, groping carefully for its bearings for fear of being engulfed in what is now the occult, the BSRA dares to explore even more vast and forbidden fields, such as the effect of mind upon matter, mental telepathy, the question of underground races, and the possibility of communicating with entities on planes of existence other than our own.

With the coming of the saucers, an interesting personage also became known to the few who could consider mediumship with an open mind, and reserve judgment on the possibility of communicating with beings outside our threshold of perception. He was Mark Probert, who began holding lengthy discourse with four "people" who seemed to be remarkably well informed on the subject of saucers, but who had the popular disadvantage of having been dead for several hundred years.

If you're already laughing, go ahead. I did myself. But to enjoy that license Layne asks only that you study his theories a bit further. Even if you can't understand some of the abstruse metaphysical principles these entities spout off now and then at garrulous moments, it will suddenly strike you that regardless of whether it is the result of fakery or the idle gossip of spirits who are as uninformed as ourselves, *the BSRA theories are the only set that can satisfactorily explain the saucer mystery.*

And now I give you the spirits, a cast of characters I limit here because of space, in order to present the more interesting ones. Unschooled in occult matters, I will not venture an explanation of just where these people are living or existing; it will perhaps suffice to say that they advise they at one time lived on Earth, were normal human beings, and now apparently are able to communicate by voice through medium Probert, while he is in deep trance:

The Yada Di' Shi'ite, an Oriental who lived 500,000 years ago in an ancient civilization in the Himalayas. He was a priest in the temple there, was killed when an earthquake destroyed the Yu civilization.

Ramon Natalli, a student of law and a close friend of the astronomer Galileo. An agnostic according to Layne, "he was pleasantly surprised to discover he had survived physical death."

Prof. Alfred Luntz, an Episcopal clergyman of England who died in 1893. Since he had preached so violently about heaven and hell, he was quite surprised to learn, upon passing, that they didn't exist.

Charles Lingford, one of the earliest entities to make contact with Probert. He was at one time a dancer and entertainer, and has a decided sense of humor. He now occupies himself mainly with music and painting, along with scientific and philosophic matters, on "the other side," where we are assured exist great libraries and other impressive sights.

Saucerians, according to these informants, are not interplanetary visitors, as we would ordinarily consider that principle, but rather superior entities who exist in other dimensions of matter—a fourth dimension, if you choose to call it that. The BSRA prefers to call these entities "etherians" and their saucers "ether ships."

It is difficult for the "controls," as the ghostly communicators are known, to explain such a complicated principle; in reading their messages one is not so sure that they, themselves, can explain or understand the complete set of concepts involved. Perhaps they do, but it is difficult to phrase them in language humans can understand.

We ordinarily think of matter, say a piece of iron or a table leg, as very much solid. In reality, scientists will tell you, such matter is first made up of molecules, then of smaller particles, atoms. Although we think of atoms as being very small, with their nuclei and rotating electrons packed very closely together, in reality they are not. For example, if some atoms were expanded, in theory, so that their electrons became the size of the Earth, the distance between the various electrons making up the atoms would be as far apart as, for example, Mars and Venus. So in relation to the size of the components, spaces within an atom are so vast it taxes the understanding to consider them.

So, in reality, explain the controls, our matter is made up from the kind of atoms we know are quite rarefied. Now picture another kind of matter that is much denser, because the components of the atoms are vibrating at a higher rate of speed. Such matter would be able to pass right through ours, with the same ease that wind or water would flow through a screen with meshes a mile wide. As an example, one might picture a ghost going smack through a stone wall—if, of course, there be ghosts. Since such matter, because of the higher vibratory rate, is beyond our range of perception, different worlds, all vibrating at different rates, can exist right alongside and interpenetrating our own, without our being aware of them.

The etherians belong to dimensions of "high" but varying densities, and it is they who are piloting most of the saucers, according to Layne and his informants. Although they have never lived on the Earth in human bodies, except under rare circumstances, they consider themselves akin to humans and all other entities that have the power of reasoning and a certain amount of intelligence.

Because of their greater scientific and mental advancement they can enter our plane of perception whenever they choose, by the process of changing their vibrational rates. When the rate of vibration is lowered to that of ours, they became visible to us, along with their flying saucers. All this could also be called, popularly, materialization and dematerialization, or, as it is abbreviated by Layne, "mat" and "demat."

Many saucer sighting accounts, which report the UFO's changing shape mysteriously or suddenly vanishing, become less puzzling when the theory of "mat" and "demat" is applied.

American and British Air Force Intelligence officers may have remembered the theory as they studied a log book of Captain James Howard, pilot of a British Overseas Airways Corporation airliner bound from New York to London. The book described seven weird black flying objects that trailed the plane for 80 miles on June 30, 1954, near Goose Bay, Labrador.

The strange story of what he and his crew and some of his passengers witnessed 19,000 feet over the Atlantic is preserved in Captain Howard's log book:

"At 0105 G.M.T. on June 30 about 150 nautical miles southwest of Goose Bay, height 19,000 feet, flying in clear weather above a layer of low cloud, noticed on our port beam a number of dark objects at approximately the same altitude as our aircraft. I drew the attention of the first officer to them. He said he had just noticed them too."

Captain Howard then saw they were moving along on a track roughly parallel to the plane and keeping the same speed.

Goose Bay radioed there were no other aircraft in the area. It was 0107 G.M.T. as the log book continued:

"During this time *the shape of the large object changed slightly* (Italics mine—G.B.), also the position of the smaller ones relative to the big one. Some moved ahead, some behind. The first officer then told Goose Bay what we were watching and they said they would send a fighter to investigate."

The large object continued to change shape, as the entire group still moved along with the plane, at a distance of about five miles or possibly much more, Howard estimated. The crew also watched the objects.

"All were agreed they never saw anything like it before. At about 0120 G.M.T. the fighter reported he was approaching and *the objects immediately began to grow indistinct until only one was visible.* This grew smaller and finally vanished at 0123 G.M.T., still at the same bearings from us."

Captain Howard described the large object to intelligence officers as like "a flying jellyfish." He also said the smaller objects kept station around the larger machine like a group of fighters acting as a bomber escort. Once the large object "looked like a dart, at another time a dumbbell," Captain Howard reported.

Lee Boyd, the co-pilot, said, "I am willing to swear that what we saw was something solid, something maneuverable, and something that was being controlled intelligently." What puzzled him, however, was the unbelievable ability of the large object to change shape.

"I have flown 7,500 hours," Captain Howard told an English representative of *The Saucerian*, "and I am certain these objects did not represent a mirage, as some officials have tried to

183

explain them away. I have seen all sorts of mirages at high altitudes, and I know them when I see them.

"One most puzzling aspect of the encounter with the objects was their strange facility of changing configuration rapidly."

BSRA theory might also explain radar sightings that cannot be confirmed visually and the weird thing five employees of the McDonnell Aircraft Corp. plant saw while going to work near St. Louis, Missouri, on July 14, 1954. It was an irregularly-shaped milky-white cloudlike substance, described as about two feet across and a foot thick. They saw the weird amorphous mass near the ground, from a distance of about 200 feet. It was traveling at slow speed, made no noise, hopped over or swerved around objects such as automobiles and fences, exited by making a sharp right turn and climbing into an overcast sky.

If saucers can materialize and dematerialize, perhaps they can also half-materialize or half-dematerialize, depending on the "side" from which one is looking. Maybe the amorphous object was only halfway onto our threshold of perception.

But, some people may counter, saucers have been seen close up, and have even been touched and found to be absolutely solid. Therefore they could not have been four-dimensional. This factor does not weaken the "4-D" theory, the BSRA claims.

The etheric counterpart of our own steel, after the vibratory rate is converted to that of our own, appears and feels absolutely solid—perhaps it is even more solid than our own steel!

But at the whim of the etherian operator, the BSRA states, the steel can be converted back to etheric or "4-D" matter, disappearing before one's eyes! Thus the theory tends to tie in with tales of saucers that disappear, or travel noiselessly through our atmosphere at fantastic speeds which would melt ordinary metal. Because etheric matter, utterly unlike our matter, is subject to the play of subtle forces, as the power of the mind, Layne further adds that most of the saucers are constructed *simply by thinking about them.*

Where do the etherians come from? Since their world can be considered coexistent with our own, maybe one is right there in the room with you now, on the bus, or wherever you happen to be reading this. But many of them originate not on Venus (as we would normally consider that planet as a physical state), but on *the etheric counterpart of Venus.* They also come from other planets, and from even beyond the Milky Way, considering these locations on the same non-materialistic basis.

Traveling such vast distances faster than even the speed of light is no trick at all, for they can transport themselves through space by merely *believing* they are at some particular location, and willing the fact into existence, so to speak.

This is akin to, though not quite the same thing, as teleportation, which some mediums have made graphically convincing, at least to some people. By the phenomenon of teleportation, an object, such as a vase for instance, can be made to vanish from one place and turn up some other place instantaneously, or so say the mediums. Scientifically it might be stated the atoms of the vase are disintegrated at one location and then reassembled in the identical pattern at some other location through some kind of power possessed by the mediums.

How the etherians can travel vast interstellar distances quicker than you can say "flying saucer" is enlarged upon by Layne, who points out that to these beings time and space are meaningless.

Picture, he tells us, a series of balls, one within the other, like the carved ivory balls or nested ivory eggs familiar in the Orient. Each smaller ball, though packed inside the other, can move freely and independently.

Now if you extend a radius from the center of the innermost ball to the surface of the outermost, and trace this line back in your thought from the point on the outermost ball, you will immediately see that the point where the radius passed through the surface of the *outside* ball is matched by a corresponding point on the *inside* surface of the same ball. There is also then a corresponding point on the outside and inside surfaces of the second ball, and so on to the center. Assume also, Layne asks, there is no "space between" surrounding these balls, since empty space, he says, "is a fiction."

Now let us say you are on the inside or outside surface of any of the balls and wish to travel along the imagined radius to the surface of another ball, say from the center ball to the outside. If we allow Layne's assumption that there is no space between the surfaces, there will be no space to be crossed and therefore no time will be required for the crossing. Considering these balls as space-time frames of reference, we then see that to pass from one space-time frame of reference to another is not a matter of "crossing" millions of light years of "space." Objects simply pass from one frame of reference and emerge in another.

Thus the BSRA prefers to term the crossing of space by the etherians "emergence." An object "emerges" when its energy is converted, by altering its vibratory rate. When the vibratory rate is altered to that of the matter we can see and touch, we can then see the flying disk, get inside it and even take a ride in it, as some individuals have claimed to have done, for the saucer is now constructed of matter like our own in almost every way.

186

The same theory also can explain the cases of Fortean falls, so called because writer Charles Fort collected and published accounts of such incidents. There have been many cases of objects, such as rocks, seeds, even fish, frogs and other living animals, falling from the sky. In such cases, according to Layne, there has been a spontaneous emergence of objects from the etheric plane into our own, by a conversion of vibratory rates. Since the etheric plane contains duplicates of Earth objects, many of these falling objects are tangible, visible, and often responsive to chemical analysis.

Why are the etherians here? On this point the controls disagree. The Yada Di' Shi'Ite said in 1953 that the coming of the disks portends the Sun's expanding into a super nova, which will fry the Earth to a crisp in an instant. He could not say the day nor the hour (perhaps showing more wisdom than many prophets!). He also predicted terrible earthquakes. Prof. Luntz felt they had a less urgent purpose, their business being primarily to make notes on the physical conditions of the Earth itself, as well as on the state and advancement of our scientific approach to life.

Whenever a civilization reaches a great state of advancement in every line, said Prof. Luntz, that civilization is due for decay, "or to put it better, change." When the etherians gather as much information as needed they hold it until such time as the civilization falls. And when another culture begins to rise again and has attained a certain degree of advancement, these things are handed down to the Earth people again through the channels of mystic organizations.

And so the saucerians are pictured as guardians of mankind in one sense, and merely as scientific observers or relatively uninterested bystanders in another. The controls warn that the ideas of morality held by the etherians may differ widely from ours, and that they may regard our own opinions of things much the way a man might regard a cockroach.

Not all saucerians are etherians, however. The universe is swarming with life forms of all sizes, shapes and colors, on a variety of planes. In addition to these "immaterial" beings there probably exist some really solid saucerians, existing permanently in our own plane, and who actually may come here from other physical planets.

It may be that Layne and his medium have found themselves a philosophical generalization into which they can retreat and take on all questioners, finding in the theory the answer to any query, including "Where was my husband last Saturday night?" And the writer, on unfamiliar grounds when he becomes enmeshed with mediums, can't vouch for the validity of the odd assortment of informants who give Probert messages in trance. For all I know, all this theory may be coming from Probert's subconscious, which may mean discounting its imaginative aspects, but not necessarily its erudite ones.

Some people, while conceding validity to the mediumship, will point out that humans on an astral level, or other spirits, may not know a lot more than humans residing on the physical plane in Brooklyn, New York—or that they may know much less.

But if a hypothesis seems to be workable, if only philosophically, it is certainly useful. No man has seen an atom; he can only imagine its inner workings. But the hypothesis involved has enabled him to build an atomic bomb. We still don't know what electricity actually is, but we have been able to use it to operate TV sets and other relatively harmless inventions. So if BSRA theory can explain saucers without loopholes, I, for one, am all for it—that is more than the Air Force has been able to do so far!

Meade Layne isn't a mere promoter, you can be assured of that. For one thing, there just isn't that much money involved in what he's doing. And to me he has consistently appeared to be an inquiring, open-minded and kind individual.

When and if man ever explains to himself just why he is here, who made the world and hung out the stars, we're afraid it won't be by the process of present day conventional scientific or philosophical reasoning. He will have to go farther into the occult or hidden or still little-understood realms of knowledge for that. And we don't think Meade Layne has the whole answer yet, nor does he claim that he does for that matter.

I think, however, he has hit on part of the truth, as have great religions and great philosophies in other times and at other street numbers. He has attempted, and quite well managed, to bring down to our realm of thinking some of the complex forces that mankind knows must exist somewhere somehow.

I knew that Bender could have obtained some of his theories from Layne because I knew he was familiar with BSRA literature. I was sure whatever earthshaking knowledge he had come upon had not been stated as such in BSRA publications, however, because Layne was still allowed to operate, apparently without molestation. Though come to think of it, Layne too had been acting mysteriously of late, as if he feared interference.

Was that the reason for the personal bulletin service he was establishing? In the light of the Bridgeport affair I felt sure Layne was trying to find some way to communicate with members in case he was forced to discontinue publishing.

A note of nervousness had crept into Layne's correspondence

shortly after an incident which occurred at the Muroc Air Force Base on the West Coast. An issue of the BSRA publication, *Clips Quotes and Comments,* had mentioned these landings, but seemingly after further consideration someone in the organization had "censored" the mimeographed account by marking through some of the sentences, leaving key details missing.

This *must* be getting bad, I thought. I wondered what Layne had found it prudent to withhold.

I noticed another item in the publication. Layne was suggesting that all members send in stamped self-addressed envelopes so that they might be reached quickly by first class mail *in the event BSRA publications had to suspend.*

A report from another West Coast source cued me in on what was withheld in the "censored" issue of *Clips Quotes and Comments.* I shot a hurried air mail to Layne, laying my cards on the table. I told him I already knew the outlines, and surely it would do no further harm to fill me in on the details.

His reply confirmed my other West Coast report:

"Dear Gray:

"Yes, I do know something about the 'big bad wolf'—i.e., the aeroforms at the Muroc Base. But as happens once in a great while, it would be easy to talk too much, and I shall have to ask you to regard this as *highly confidential.* By that I mean please do not at this time refer to me or the BSRA as being the *source* or authority for the statement that these craft *voluntarily* landed at the base and have been closely studied by our technicians, and inspected by President Eisenhower himself during his stay at Palm Springs.

"This story has already gotten out, as was inevitable—but is still flatly denied by the Pentagon and by all other official sources. Since I would like to keep publishing for a while, I do not wish to be publicly named as being responsible for it."

My other West Coast source had told me technicians were studying the saucers, but were almost going nuts while doing so. The strange craft were unlike anything on Earth, and represented technology far beyond present knowledge.

This was a new one, though, about a personal inspection by the President!

I had been trying to think of another news item that I had almost discarded from my mind because when I read it there seemed to be little importance in it—just the usual small talk when the paper was hard to fill up.

Then I remembered what it was about, and the implication almost staggered me. Here was confirmation from the press!

Reporters, the small item had declared, had been trying to find the President during his stay at Palm Springs, but he had completely eluded them. Apparently he wasn't really in Palm Springs, at all! Had the President only ostensibly vacationed at the resort, spending most of his time at the nearby base where his real reason for flying to the West Coast lay?

Layne had received his information through reliable sources, he felt:

"The man who first gave us this information is a highly responsible person who himself spent two days at the Base. He gave me the names of three fairly well-known persons who accompanied him, and who presumably will, at a later date, publicly verify his account. Since that time I have received corroborative evidence from two other sources. I will add, also confidentially, that within the last two to three days I have been able to enlist the active cooperation of a nationally known news commentator of a large radio network who says that he is determined to 'break this matter wide open.' (Author's note.

This radio commentator subsequently was "silenced."—G.B.)

"You will note that what I have been summing up here is quite different from the rumors in your letter to me. So far as I know, there is no truth in reports that a missile or any other UFO has been found near the state line. The objects in question consist of aeroforms of five different types, and they are said to have completely baffled scientists and 'experts.' I repeat that this comes from a most dependable eyewitness, who named three other persons of importance who accompanied him. Personally, I accept his account, and am glad to pass the substance of it on to you, under the temporary and necessary conditions mentioned above.

"It is not solely a matter of protecting our BSRA setup, but other people are involved, and I do not wish to get them into difficulty. The upshot of this whole business is, of course, obvious and inevitable—everything will have to come out, and the public will have to find out about it the hard way—as usual."

Layne's last paragraph reminded me of what Bender had said when Lucchesi asked him if the people will be told what the saucers are.

"It has got to a point where they will have to be," Bender had replied.

If Bender's information concerned the Muroc landing perhaps it had been more specific than had Layne's. Although Layne had sensed an indication he was being watched closely and that he might be prevented from publishing any day, as yet he had not been "shushed up."

Had there been contact between saucer people and officials at the Base? Had Bender got wind of some of the things learned

192

from the saucer people? That would have been "big," all right, and could have led to the statement in Bender's letter.

Bender had told Jarrold, "Something big has taken place over here, and we cannot reveal it at this time for fear of the results."

In a later communication Bender said, "I might add that I was terribly sick for three days after I saw those three men and also frightened beyond reason."

I asked myself the question: If I found out the end of the world was impending would I, myself, not become ill?

I continued to read Bender's letter to Jarrold.

The visit was conducted, Bender told him, as he had reported to Lucchesi, Roberts and me, by three men, "all dressed in black suits," but he added to the Australian investigator that they "showed credentials."

It all came about because of something he had written in a thesis and submitted to a "certain person."

"I found out," Bender stated, "that I had stumbled upon something that I was not supposed to know." When the three men told Bender "a certain bit of information" he said, "I think I got white as a ghost."

He told Jarrold he was on his honor as a citizen of the United States to remain silent.

It was embarrassing, he said, to find himself in such a position. He had been forced to turn down 70 new memberships to IFSB within the past few days. Jarrold, he added, could quote freely from *Space Review* in the next issue of *The Australian Flying Saucer Magazine,* if, as he put it, Jarrold *decided to publish one.*

What was the terrifying information Bender had discovered? Other investigators could only guess. The following questions were never answered, but they contain a clue to the possibilities Fulton was considering at the time. He sent them in the form of a questionnaire, hoping Bender could answer at least those questions which would not infringe upon his vows.

(1) Were your visitors United States authority?

(2) Were your visitors interplanetary authority?

(3) Is the answer to the saucers interplanetary?

(4) Is the planet Mars the home base of the saucers?

(5) Was your sickness due to the nature of the saucer beings and suspect purposes thereof?

(6) Have the United States authorities in effect forbidden civilian investigation of saucers through their visit to you?

(7) Is there a race between a number of interplanetary beings to establish themselves on Earth?

(8) Are our visitors from space virtually in control?

(9) Is the answer interdimensional, astral or etherical?

(10) Are your thoughts exposed to reception or does telepathic communication play a leading part?

Bender had one answer to all of Fulton's questions. Perhaps he realized that by a slow accumulation of answers to leading questions his secret could eventually be discovered, if only by the process of elimination.

And Bender was scared. Scared that he would slip. He didn't want another visit from the three men.

One time he *had* made a slip during a long distance phone conversation, he told Fulton. As soon as the phone was hung up it rang again. Someone from Washington was on the line this time. The party warned Bender to be careful.

Bender's answer to Fulton's ten-part question was contained in one sentence appended to the list of queries and returned:

"The above questions are not to be answered due to security reasons."

The new files on Bender read like the progress of the mystery from my end. Sooner or later there would be a suppressed shudder from Jarrold, as he made the final deduction—and then wished he could wipe it from his mind.

On November 3 he sent a worried letter to Fulton.

He had reviewed all of his IFSB correspondence, had come to certain conclusions about the dissolving of the American organization and Bender's odd behavior. He felt sure that he knew the "principal facts."

Ever since that startling realization had hit him he had been upset, hoping tremendously that the interpretation he made was a lot of nonsense. But as the pieces fell together into a disquieting pattern he could see it was not absurd.

It explained Bender's behavior and experiences, left only a small margin of doubt.

"I informed Mr. Bender to that effect the very next day after making the deduction, feeling the course a definite duty. Since then, *for very strong and vital reasons*, the information has not been divulged to anyone else."

Jarrold didn't know what to do with the knowledge since he considered it "highly dangerous."

"At the moment the matter—for reasons which cannot be discussed—must remain at that until positive information is at hand from other sources. Believe me when I say that *no one hopes more than I do that the interpretation of certain material is wrong.* Since making the deduction I have been more worried than I care to say and at first *wished I had never undertaken saucer research.*"

Here was a statement similar to the one Jarrold had published in the November, 1953, issue of his *The Australian Flying Saucer Magazine.* The man was frightened. No doubt about that.

What had he run across? It indeed sounded portentous.

Whatever the theory was, Bender was no help to Jarrold, and the latter remained in as much befuddlement about the American investigator as the rest of us.

But Bender had given him some advice:

"If you have found out the mystery of the saucers, for heaven's sake, do not get yourself into trouble over it."

Bender and Jarrold, I thought, must have found out the same thing. And now Jarrold was apparently silenced by a mysterious visitor who perhaps had confirmed the very thing he suspected.

I now had the answers, perhaps, if I could put them together.

If I could forge the images of Bender and Jarrold into some kind of mental thaumatrope and in the spinning image coalesce the causes of their fears, maybe I, myself, could arrive at their conclusion.

Maybe I would be happier if I remained in ignorance.

XIII

Outside U.S.A.

Try to make sense out of the saucer riddle and—unless you are Bender or Jarrold—you draw a blank. There are too many loose ends. Can saucers have anything to do with a mysterious telephone call in which you talk to an unearthly, frighteningly distinct voice, or a pair of moccasins that walks although nobody is in them?

Probably not.

Yet, can one be sure?

Time after time, a clue appears, is eagerly followed up, and leads to a dead end, contributing only to the elusiveness and bewilderment of the mystery. Perhaps I am only adding ambiguity by relating chronicles that are necessarily undocumented, because those who have experienced them are now locked in silence.

You would like this book better if it gave you all the answers. It would be fairly easy to do, to give you answers. Answers that might satisfy some of you.

I could draw conclusions and twist my facts to fit them. I could make some of you who do not have time to check the facts think I'm a big boy. I could leave enough holes in my theories to give me room for escape should my major premise ever be invalidated.

But I don't like theories which are finalized.

I could satisfy many of you, but I couldn't satisfy myself.

*   *   *   *   *

Since Bender could no longer discuss the saucer mystery, there was little point in keeping in close touch with him. Then I knew he must be busy with preparations for his forthcoming marriage. I respected his alleged pledge to reveal nothing of what he had learned, but giving him up as a source of information did not mean the end of my search. There should be other avenues through which I could attack the problem.

Maybe I would run across someone else who had been visited, or "shushed up." By learning more about their experiences, perhaps I could fit more pieces to the puzzle.

I found another person. And in finding him, I found a partly familiar setting, a recurring clue.

Something that fell out of the skies. Some slag-like residue. And a visitor.

Again, in the background of a mystery, jigsaw puzzle pieces

that seem to fit and yet fall apart as fast as you can find adjacencies.

I don't know quite how to tell this man's story for I cannot give you his name. Perhaps I could assign one to him. I like people with names. It gives them presence, reality, invests them in flesh and blood, as they swirl in a maelstrom of the abstract, the unsolved, and the unknown.

I would like to know someone by the name of Gordon Smallwood. The name in itself sounds honest and reputable. If there are any Gordon Smallwoods reading this book, let them rest assured the name used here is an invention. But let them write to me for I would like to know people with such a name.

The man I am about to tell you of, however, is no invention. There is a reason I cannot use his name. The man is frightened.

I will not mention the country in which Gordon Smallwood, as I shall call him, resides. It is not the United States, but it is near. Smallwood is not a native of the country I cannot name.

I am permitted to tell you he is a Latvian, from one of the Baltic states now under Russian occupation. He came to his present homeland from Europe in 1947. He is now 35 years old.

Smallwood is an assayer for a gold mine, but he hopes some day to be able to continue the study of architecture begun in his former homeland and interrupted by the Germans, who arrested him for underground activities.

"I have had a pretty hard life," he once commented.

And, one might add, an exciting one.

Anyone who had survived the terrors of the underground would not frighten easily, I mused, asking myself, as I read Smallwood's communication, why such a person would be terrified and made ill by the visit of a man who threatened him.

"Things are different now," he explained. "I wouldn't worry about myself. It's my wife and child."

The quiet beginning of the story belies the terror that will soon permeate it.

A man (not Smallwood) is spending his vacation in a summer camp. He is on the river, his fishing lines are in the water. He sits back, lazily watching cloud formations.

His attention is diverted by something that darts into view from behind the clouds, then hovers over the bushes along the shore. He can't estimate exactly the altitude to which the object has descended, though it is probably between 400 and 1,000 feet.

The cigar-shaped object hovers there for about ten seconds, and then flies off. While the fisherman is still staring in amazed bewilderment he hears a noise (the object itself has made none) that sounds as if something were falling into the bushes.

He rows ashore. There he spies a metallic-looking substance, lying about on the ground, some of it collected on the brush. He picks up a bit of it, cautiously, for somehow he feels it should be hot. To his surprise it is ice cold, as cold as the inside of a freezer—and yet the substance is quite dry. He collects a quantity of it in a paper bag and takes it back to camp with him.

Smallwood heard a rumor of the occurrence, and through a great deal of inquiry in the vicinity finally located the individual.

"I don't want to get in trouble," the camper protested, when Smallwood asked for some of the material and quizzed him for details. The vacationer believed the aerial object was some sort of guided missile being tested by the government. Finally, after Smallwood had convinced him the object did not behave as a guided missile should behave, and promised to keep his name in absolute confidence, he parted with a sample of the metallic substance and described the sighting in full detail.

Smallwood sent a sample of the metallic substance to a well-known testing laboratory in a nearby metropolis. His own equipment was inadequate for making a complete analysis. He did check the substance with a Geiger counter; a slight radioactivity was registered.

Hearing this report from Smallwood, I was curious about the outcome of the analysis, and having received no word for about a month, directed an inquiry to him.

I received no reply, figured Smallwood must have become busy with some project and was forced to neglect his correspondence.

About six weeks later he sent a letter which was to deepen my curiosity even further, and lead me to fear for his safety.

Let me quote from this letter in part:

"Excuse the long silence. I know you have been waiting for some news concerning the fragments and the analysis, but I hope that you'll understand (at least partly) the reasons for my silence.

"During the last two weeks so much happened that I was unable to write even a short letter. Most of the happenings were of very unpleasant nature, leaving me with a nervous breakdown. My recent activities have caused much trouble for another person and his family. When it all started I made promises to myself, promises that I would never again fool around with saucers, and for a while I even felt as if I wanted to burn all my files, photographs and correspondence on the subject. This might sound quite strange to you, but I'm not sure about what you yourself would have done had you been in my skin at that time.

"Today it all looks different to me. I'm not as frightened; I'm just mad that I was foolish enough to play at being a serious 'investigator.' There are certain limits in which an ordinary fellow can go—then he must stop and leave the further road for others to walk on. These others are more 'serious and experienced' than I am and they know their 'business.' I am merely a child of 34 years.

"As to the fragments, I cannot promise any further news concerning the affair. I'm sorry, Gray, really sorry. Isn't it strange that a man will do everything in order to solve some mystery and later loses all interest in it when he finds out the mystery isn't for him to fool around with?

"As I said before, I had decided to drop everything concerning saucers, including correspondence, but after cool consideration, I changed my mind. Who can tell me to quit collecting reports or writing letters to my friends? Nobody, I hope. . . .

"Be very careful, Gray, if you happen to investigate some new report."

You can imagine my surprise—and concern—when I read the letter. Smallwood sounded as if he had been "visited." I wondered if it tied in with the Bridgeport three-men-deal.

If so, it appeared that when the visitors came there was no talking thereafter! What methods did these visitors utilize to so terrorize saucer investigators?

Smallwood lives a long way from Clarksburg, but I picked up the telephone and in about an hour had him on the other end. Perhaps I could get a better picture of just what had happened.

"Tell me what you can, Gordon," I begged of him. "It may be important to my finding out some other things."

He still sounded scared, but did not talk at all abnormally. When I received the letter I feared my correspondent might have "gone off his rocker," but this suspicion was soon allayed when I heard his friendly, joking voice.

"Don't let it worry you too much, Gray," he assured me. "It's probably not too important. And I can't tell you the details —although I'd like to more than you realize."

"Is it the three-men-deal?" I asked, knowing he was familiar with the Bender matter since we had often discussed it.

"Not three men, *one* man," Smallwood replied. "As far as I know it had nothing to do with Bender's troubles."

It was established Smallwood *had* been visited, and I soon learned the visitor had been from his government, though he would not say which branch was involved. The visitor had taken the sample of metallic material in Smallwood's possession and then had given him certain "advice," as Smallwood put it in talking to me on the phone. The "advice" didn't specifically call for Smallwood to give up saucer research, but from the way Smallwood talked to me I gathered that the visitor had been far from approving of this activity.

No, the visitor did not disclose anything about the saucer mystery. He was concerned mainly with the material and the analysis, warning Smallwood not to talk about the latter.

I asked if he had received an analysis of the substance from the laboratory to which he had submitted a sample. Yes, said Smallwood, caught off guard; its main constituent was titanium, and the other constituents were also relatively common metals and metallic compounds. He knew this before his visitor came.

Giving me this information was a slip Smallwood evidently regretted. Immediately, he insisted that I publish nothing about any part of the affair, and especially not about the analysis, in *The Saucerian*, and most emphatically not in connection with his name.

That was all I could get from him, and I had a vision of the toll charges mounting on my bill at the telephone office. So I hung up.

Smallwood couldn't figure out where the visitor might have learned about his submission of the sample to the laboratory, because he said he knew the laboratory hadn't given out any information about it. Smallwood wondered if any of his friends had reported the matter to the government.

Another letter, however, received about six weeks later, began to fill me in on some of the points which had puzzled me, and I wondered if Smallwood might tell me even more if I approached him again.

"As far as my last year's troubles are concerned," Smallwood's January 20, 1955, letter informed me, "I am afraid I cannot tell you much. All the affair is more fantastic than I ever dreamed and if I tried to talk about it, I would be placed on the same shelf so many people I regard as crackpots occupy."

It was running true to form, I decided: it seemed that after a visit that word "fantastic" usually cropped up. I wondered if it could connote anything supernatural, or if the visit had revealed some unusual situation, such as, for example, the development of some radical new type of aircraft. It was also true to form that the visitor had returned for a second "chat."

"I was plain stupid when the visitor came to see me for the first time, but I was much smarter when he returned."

Then a bombshell that confirmed my suspicions:

"The man wasn't representing what I thought him to be representing. There is certainly no government agency involved, and I don't have to be afraid to spill the whole matter. That is, I don't have to be afraid of the ———, ——— or police (Smallwood mentioned two government police agencies operating in his country). But the man who came to see me threatened me very openly and advised me not to tell anyone about the results of the analysis. Now I have given sealed envelopes to several of my friends to be opened in case something happens to me. These envelopes contain the results of the analysis and a story of the whole affair."

Smallwood, always a materialist, apparently did not connect the supernatural with his visit, though several friends to whom he had told some of the story did.

"Two friends of mine quit corresponding with me because they fear some mysterious underground entities and believe that it is dangerous to be in contact with me since I'm a 'marked man.' Yes, Gray, I'm not fooling, so don't laugh. Crazy world, eh! After all, we saucer lunatics are not the worst bunch among the cranks!

"I'm really very sorry that I can't tell you more."

If the visitor was not from Smallwood's government, I reasoned, what agency could he represent? Were private individuals engaged in suppressing the facts? Were certain agencies, opposed to saucer investigation, operating?

If I could interview Smallwood personally I felt sure I could settle some of my questions, for he seemed less afraid to talk than Bender had been. Going to see him was out of the question. So I hit upon preparing a questionnaire that might tell me what I wanted to know by simple "yes" and "no" answers.

Smallwood, however, was more informative than I had hoped, for he enlarged considerably upon the expected answers.

Q. Did the visitor contact you a total of two times?

A. Yes.

Q. Did the visitor contact you only one time?

A. No.

Q. Did the visitor contact you more than one time?

A. Yes.

Q. At the time I telephoned you had you then been visited only one time?

A. Yes.

Q. If the answer to the above is "yes," did you, at the time I telephoned you, believe the visitor was from your government?

A. Yes. During the second visit he insisted that he represented a certain government agency which I will not name, but during his first visit I was so scared that I never asked him to show his credentials. His conversation was rather pleasant during that visit, and he appeared to be very kind, excepting some hints he gave me regarding my activities and the possible consequences. But you should have seen his face, during the second visit, when I asked him to produce his credentials and identify himself. His attitude changed instantly, and he became so threatening I was immediately convinced that no man, sent by that agency, would act in that manner.

Q. Did the visitor represent an extraterrestrial agency?

A. I don't know.

206

Q. Did the visitor represent what might be termed an "esoteric agency" of Earth?

A. I don't know.

Q. Did the visitor represent a foreign power (foreign terrestrial power such as, but not necessarily, Russia)?

A. For a while I had the feeling the man might be a Communist, but his later conversation convinced me he was not.

Q. Did the visitor threaten bodily or any other harm?

A. I'll try to give you an example of his threats. I cannot be sure that I remember his words correctly, but the following will give you an idea if he meant bodily harm or not. "Your recent activities are very, very (I remember he said "very" twice) undesirable and if they are continued, they might be dangerous to you and your family. We (he always used "we") would like to advise you to cease all your activities connected with these fragments. Our second advice is to forget that such things as flying saucers exist." There were other threats, but I would not like to talk about them.

Q. Do you feel your visitor was from the same agency which sent the three men to visit Bender?

A. My information concerning the Bender affair does not go beyond what I read in *The Saucerian* and a few other publications of similar nature. I was corresponding with Bender before the closing of his organization, but knew nothing about what led to its end.

Q. Did the visitor impart any frightening information to you?

A. No.

Q. Did a discussion about the South Pole come up?

A. I'll answer this one by asking you a question. Why do

you include a question about the South Pole with the others? I can understand all of them except this one.

Q. Does the matter have anything to do with the Shaver Mystery?

A. I don't know.

Q. You said in a letter the man had threatened you. If so why don't you go to the police?

A. What kind of protection can police offer me, even if they believe my story and check it? Place a couple of husky body-guards outside my door? For how long? I'm very much afraid that police protection cannot be very effective in this case, but I have taken the necessary steps to make sure that information concerning the fragments reaches authorities in case my visitor shows intention of fulfilling his threats. As far as I understand it, the most important factor in this affair is the matter of the fragments and the analysis thereon. As long as I keep my mouth shut about this, I believe no harm will come to me.

Q. Are your thoughts exposed to telepathic communication?

A. This question makes me laugh, Gray! What was the idea to include this one? Do you really think I'm cracking up or what?

Smallwood didn't realize it, but the last question was one of the most helpful of the lot. I was glad he answered it so sanely, for his response made me surer than ever before that the thing had actually happened to Smallwood and that he was on the level.

I was happy Smallwood felt it was safe to give me a description of the visitor, although he said he didn't see how this would help me solve the saucer mystery. The visitor was ordinary in appearance, quite tall, with black hair. He wore a dark gray overcoat, white shirt and blue tie with some kind of stripes (Smallwood did not say whether his clothing was the same color on both visits, or if this description referred to what he wore on only one occasion).

One striking note about the man's appearance did impress Smallwood, however.

His face, neck and hands were deeply tanned.

"It wasn't the kind of tan you get after spending a month or two in Florida. It was tan you have all the year due to constant exposure to the sunlight. And somehow I'm sure all of his skin was that color."

Smallwood said I probably wondered if he had tried to trace the man after he left the house.

"While he was sitting in my living room, I left him for a while and went into another room where my wife was, asked her to get dressed and follow the man in order to see where he went, or to obtain the number of his license plates if he were driving a car.

"He walked down the street to a hotel and entered the lobby, from which he walked upstairs. Because he didn't use the elevator my wife deduced he was living on one of the lower floors. She telephoned me, asked me to come to the hotel.

"She waited until I had arrived, then returned home. I waited for another half hour, then asked the clerk if such a man was a guest in the hotel. I gave the fellow a detailed description of the man, but he was positive that no such person had registered. Only about 30 guests were in the hotel at that time, and half of those were permanent tenants. The other half were people the clerk knew by name and most of them were not staying at the hotel for the first time.

"So there I was—like a dog that had lost the trail. I waited for another hour and went home. I am unable to explain the disappearance."

XIV

New Zealand

Bender had not discontinued *Space Review* immediately. He published a few additional issues, but a great change had come over it. No saucers!

The first issue in new dress concerned Mars and the forthcoming favorable opposition in the summer of 1954. But when I picked up the August, 1954, issue I wasn't so sure Bender was completely silent about what he had found out.

Bender, in his article titled "True Or False Statements," might be trying to tell something.

All books and magazines which publish material on saucers

mix true statements with false, he declared, and only the reader skilled in decoding double talk can tell the one from the other. Then came a challenge to his subscribers: five "explanations" which might be sound or unsound, he pointed out, but which would all be presented with equal seriousness.

Did the statements which followed include one or two in particular which represented the startling secret Bender was forced to keep? By sandwiching this information in with deliberate fiction, might he have found a way to get the gnawing secret off his chest for the moment, with no fear of reprisal from the three men?

Do not assume that these paragraphs hold the answer; Bender may merely have been trying to throw civilian investigators off the track. But here is the sense of his five "explanations," presented for what they may be worth:

1. A base on the moon, set up and controlled by the United States, has been in operation for more than seven years. Part of the operating cost of this base is diverted from the sums earmarked for atom research. There are regular contacts between the lunar base and bases on Earth; news of the base has not leaked out because it has been staffed with personnel who had no home ties.

2. The Russians are on the moon. They are building launching sites for super-rockets; their aim is global domination. The targets of their super-rockets will of course be the democratic nations.

3. Some world power—unnamed—has perfected a device surpassing any known type of aircraft.

4. Our own government possesses a secret so extraordinary that those in authority fear to make it public knowledge.

5. The Russians are planning a new type of warfare, in which

the enemy will not be eliminated by death. Instead, guided circular objects will spread an overpowering gas over enemy territory. Anyone breathing the gas will be put to sleep, and while all the citizens of a country are immobilized, the Russians will take over the reins of government.

Which—if any—of these explanations bears a relation to Bender's visit from three mysterious men?

* * * * *

By this time Fulton had decided to send me the details on "Project X," since no breach of confidence would now be involved. After all, thought Fulton, it looked as if Bender had completely divorced himself from saucer research, was no longer concerned with it.

Bender had suggested to Jarrold and him that "Project X" be formed.

Shortly after their experiences with the strange bangings and odors they had apprised Bender of the occurrences. Bender had answered somewhat cryptically.

He took a serious view of the events and gave some strange advice. They were to watch their files carefully, for "any material which may disappear."

Had someone or something taken material from Bender's own files? He didn't enlarge on his statement.

Bender noted the many sightings in the Australia and New Zealand area.

"I have wondered about a theory of an organization here in the United States that believes the source of the saucers is the Antarctic. If this were true it might account for the numerous sightings in your locale, and the mysterious actions of July 21 and 22. They are probably nearer to you than you realize."

So "Project X" *did* concern Antarctica, as I had guessed.

Jarrold suggested that he and Fulton investigate the possibilities of an Antarctic saucer base. Jarrold could conceive of such a base, for one strong reason. It would be relatively free from human observation. It would be the perfect spot for such headquartering, provided the entities involved could survive the intense cold, or had a way of shielding themselves from it. Or did not need to, if the temperature there were similar to that of their home planet.

If a space ship from Earth were to land on Mars, for example, and find a highly-developed civilization there, the first move probably would be to observe the civilization from a distance before it could be determined if public landing was safe. The explorers would select a remote section of the planet, away from the prying eyes (or whatever they look with) of the Martians, on which to locate their base. They would then make exploratory trips over the populated areas, often landing to collect samples of flora, fauna and soil.

The Martians would observe the alien craft, but those who were concerned, who wrote and spoke about the phenomena would be labeled "pfhagrhrrrtphphs," which is probably the Martian equivalent of "crack-pots."

Sooner or later some of the pfhagrhrrrtphphs would get together to compare notes. They would publish magazines about their findings. Three Martians might even visit them and shut them up.

Someone sooner or later would get the idea of plotting the courses of the strange craft. If the crafts' movements were found to have a standard pattern, then mapping each arrival and departure might point to the place they were coming from—might reveal the location of their secret base.

That is what Jarrold and Fulton decided to do.

It would be a big task, for it involved going through thousands of reports, many of which did not clearly state the direction of arrival or departure. They would first sort out those reports which stated directions clearly, then determine two points from each account:

1. The approximate directions from which the objects came.
2. The approximate directions of their departure.

The directions of arrival and departure would be drawn on a map projection as a series of lines. If many of the lines had a tendency to intersect in any certain area, that might indicate the location of a base or rendezvous point for the craft!

They would enlist the help of the IFSB, and if all the findings jibed they felt they would have something real and concrete to present to their specific governments and to the press.

But immediately after this proposal was in Bender's hands he informed the world he could no longer have anything to do with the saucer mystery.

Fulton believed it would be wise to soft pedal the Antarctic theory until things quieted down in Bridgeport. Maybe that had been the straw that would have broken the back of the mystery, the theory that brought the three men on the double. Bender's strange actions, coupled with Jarrold's concentration on his own disturbing theories and his subsequent visit from an enigmatic caller postponed the investigation indefinitely.

To my present knowledge "Project X" still remains in Fulton's files for future action. He has never followed it through.

Fulton's interest in the mystery of Bridgeport was to ebb lower as the puzzle continued to remain unsolved. He had many other tasks to perform, since the membership of his organization was growing. Jarrold's communications were to become less frequent and more cryptic, until at last they trickled into a dead silence.

If some were frightened into silence, others surged forward to take their places. One such organization was Flying Saucer Investigators of Hamilton, New Zealand, a small group which chose to remain that way. Its founders, John E. Stuart and Doreen A. Wilkinson, felt that a few sincere investigators could accomplish much if membership were limited and administrative details thus minimized.

Every week John and Doreen, as they wanted me to address them informally, met in his home, where they analyzed and answered the correspondence always piling up and forwarded their findings to other groups.

One day I sent them what I considered a rather startling and puzzling enclosure. It was about another investigator far from Bridgeport, Connecticut. It was the copy of a letter from a man frightened half to death, intimidated by a mysterious visitor who had demanded that he turn over a certain piece of metal. You have read about this man in Chapter Thirteen, where I called him Gordon Smallwood.

I copied the letter and sent it to a few select investigators who had been working with me on the Bender mystery. I thought it might fit in. I demanded and received their fullest confidence, for Smallwood feared at the time that public knowledge of his experience might result in bodily harm to him.

After John and Doreen read the puzzling letter they thought it was time they should be telling me about some of their own experiences. They had remained silent for fear people might scoff.

Their tale was fantastic.

It had occurred two years before that spring of 1954.

John went to bed early that night, around 9:30. He wasn't asleep, though, when the telephone rang at 11:30, for he was trying to finish a book he had purchased a few days before.

It was rather late for a telephone call, and there was almost annoyance in his voice when he answered it.

"Are you John Stuart?"

Yes, he replied that was correct.

"You are the John Stuart who is interested in what Earth men call 'flying saucers.' "

The voice put it more like a statement than a question. John noted an odd monotone about the voice, as if some kind of machine had learned how to talk.

"You are quite correct," John answered. "Just what can I do for you?"

"I warn you to stop interfering in matters that do not concern you!"

John got angry. He appreciated a good joke as well as anyone, but not at any hour of the night.

"Who is this?" he demanded.

"I am .... from another planet."

John couldn't remember the name, which sounded unpronounceable. He replied to the voice with the New Zealand equivalent of "You and who else?"

"You have been warned," the voice said. Then a click and the "otherworldly" conversation was terminated.

John got up and poured himself a drink. Of course it had to be a practical joker, but he couldn't be sure. One thing was peculiar, he noted. Usually he could hear noises on the line, such as the faint click of other numbers being dialed, but the voice had come through without the usual background sounds.

It had remarkable volume, compared with other telephone conversations.

It was with trepidation that John and Doreen, who wrote their letters jointly, told me of their disquieting experiences, for they feared I would think the mystery was getting the best of them. Nevertheless John went on to tell me more.

"It was about a year ago that another odd thing occurred. The hour was late and I was standing in the lounge doorway smoking a cigarette. I was only four feet away from the front door—and this is important, Gray—facing that way. Suddenly I heard footsteps on the concrete path outside. The sound made me wonder who would be calling so late at night. The doorbell rang. I went to the door, opened it (quickly after the ring, for I was on the way to the door already upon hearing the approach of the visitor), and there was no one there!

"I ran outside, hoping to catch what obviously must be a prankster. Everything was silent. Whoever or whatever it was did not have time to get away without my observation.

"I still think this has no supernatural connotation, but Doreen isn't so sure."

John himself had heard the odd sounds Doreen then reported to me.

"I too have had some strange experiences similar to John's," she advised.

"The first time I noticed anything untoward happening was something like three months ago. John and I were having a meeting which I interrupted to go out after some cigarettes. When I returned to the house I put my cycle against the hedge, went up to the porch. Just as I was about to open the door I heard an odd shuffling sound, as though someone were half dragging his feet along in soft soled shoes, something like some-one wearing a pair of bedroom slippers two or three sizes too large. I looked toward the sound behind me. There was absolutely nothing there! When I turned the noise stopped; when I turned back again to open the door it resumed. It then seemed to come from the back of the house along the path. I entered and told John, 'There's someone out there.' He investigated but could find no one, but could hear the strange noise, then moving toward the gate."

They were still afraid I would think reports of bizarre happenings other researchers said they had experienced were making them "jumpy." Now that I had already formed my opinion of their imaginations, they said, almost petulantly, they might as well give me all of it.

Just one week before something else had happened.

About 9:30 P.M. on their meeting night they were preparing to quit their work when Doreen heard a sound "like someone breathing deeply." She looked at John, who was bent over the desk, examining a newspaper clipping. It wasn't he, for it was coming from the other side of the room! No one else was present, her somewhat uneasy glance around the room disclosed.

Doreen said she must be up early the next morning, and John walked with her to the gate. While they stood talking for a moment she heard something.

"Crunch! crunch! crunch!"

That was as closely as she could describe the sound. It was coming from the road, as if an invisible personage were walking there.

John didn't act as if he had heard it, so she didn't mention it. Surely it must be her imagination. Her bicycle ride to her home that night was a swift one, she remarked later to John, when without any prompting he had asked her if she had heard a queer noise anywhere about the house.

As Doreen cycled away that night, John could hear the crunch! crunch! crunch!" approaching him. He had seen Doreen off from the back yard. The sound of invisible walking approached and passed him, proceeded around the house. John followed the footsteps.

"Can you imagine my amazement, and, I am afraid, no little shock, when I saw the front door open and close!

"Curiosity must have overridden bravery as I leaped onto the porch and tugged at the door knob."

Then he remembered. The front door was locked, as always. He fiddled in his pocket for the key, but it wasn't there. He had left it inside. He ran around to the back of the house, entered, and made a complete search.

Nothing.

I asked the investigators if I could publish their experiences. They said they would leave it up to me.

"Being somewhat enmeshed in this thing myself, Gray," John wrote, "I know how it is to hear something and be asked to keep it a secret. I sincerely believe publication of these experiences would be of little value to saucer research, which, Doreen and I believe, should move along materialistic lines, for that is the only avenue in which one can find proper scientific standards for any analysis of findings that might be accepted generally. From your own experiences, Gray, you know things happen to all of us investigators. I think the best thing is to play them down, since there seems to be little hope of understanding them.

"As a fellow investigator I am not going to limit you to confidence. Use your judgment. I might point out that if you do publish these somewhat 'spooky' stories, few are going to believe them. If you publish them let me suggest that you play the more dramatic elements down and refrain from sensationalization."

I have gone somewhat against John's wishes and am publishing the facts as he gave them to me. In any aspect of the saucer mystery the reader has the alternative of believing or disbelieving. In publishing the information I have found no need for sensationalizing.

Maybe this has no place in a book devoted to flying saucers. Maybe it is fallacious to connect the pall of terror that hung over John's house with the mystery of the disks. Because John was concerned about the UFO's, however, there is a logical tendency, I believe, to connect the two enigmas.

If saucers had something to do with the invisible entities which chose to become his unwelcome guests, all spiritualistic phenomena may hold some puzzling relationship with saucers.

There is a terminology for the unfamiliar, and in that ghostly dictionary are numerous forces which move by night and day, here and there able to gain the power to impinge themselves on man's consciousness.

The happenings at the headquarters of Flying Saucer Investigators would likely be put down by those who deal in such matters as poltergeist activity. A poltergeist is a noisy and mischievous entity or force of some kind, which apparently gains gratification from noisy bangings, invisible walking, and, more rarely, the outpourings of unpleasant odors and materializations of puzzling nature. No one has connected poltergeists with saucers, to my knowledge, and the presence of one, if that was what the thing was, at John's house may have been only a coincidence.

But maybe his delving into the secrets of the disks had opened a door somewhere that should have remained closed, a door that would admit the unknown in all of its terrible and incomprehensible trappings.

Since the voice had told John, "You have been warned," the happenings at his house might be interpreted, by one who would put two saucers together and come up with "4-D," as a kind of ghastly persecution. A discouragement for an investigator who might be approaching truth too nearly.

After the episode of the invisible walker Doreen refused to go home alone. After returning from escorting her one evening, John sat down in the library to read. Let us offer the saucer critics an excuse, if a slight and ridiculous one, to help them gloss over and forget the incident, to allow them to explain it away.

John was drinking a glass of beer.

They will say the alcoholic content of the glass of beer clouded John's vision, and that the mellowing and intoxicating effects of the beverage led him to see, as he glanced over the top of his book, the toe piece of a moccasin jutting out over some books.

What is unusual about the toe piece of a moccasin?

Nothing—until it begins *moving*, along the row of books. John blinked and looked again. It had disappeared.

He put the book away, crediting the incident to eye strain. Then he glanced toward the front of the room. There was the entire pair of moccasins, as if someone were standing in them, by the fireplace!

"They seemed to be made of a coarse but closely-woven brownish material, almost the color of khaki."

John slowly arose to walk toward them. Suddenly they were gone!

But still he didn't take the advice of the mysterious telephone caller. He persisted in saucer investigation.

Later he was to wish he hadn't.

XV

Clarksburg, West Virginia

The summer of 1954.

Although the H-bomb and Congressional committees were in the forefront of attention, saucer enthusiasts who kept their eyes turned toward the heavens could see many things—and wondered why the newspapers would not (or could not) report what they were witnessing.

Saucers seemed to be everywhere. But the Air Force continued with its Fact Sheets, its occupation with weather balloons, hallucinations and "natural phenomena," apparently disregarding hundreds of sightings reported each week. I looked at the ever-growing pile of mail on my own desk and shrugged: there were so many saucers in the skies that to list only the unusual or spectacular ones would take hundred-page issues of *The Saucerian*—pages I did not have.

And the summer wore on into August, a summer that was not quite right. There were more freak weather conditions and earthquakes, and in the air were threats of something unknown that was to come. Windshields broke mysteriously from coast to coast. There were hints that astronomers had focused their telescopes close to Earth, peering at something they could not explain. A second moon, perhaps, but more likely something else: an artificial satellite, some hinted, but *not ours*.

Meanwhile man threatened man and there were wars and rumors of wars. But to those who could feel it, there was something else, a half-heard rumbling in the air, like a bad dream, as the world whirled deliriously onward in what seemed to some to be a mad phantasmagoria of the dance of death.

Whatever it was, it would come. One had the impression that something was being sat upon, that there were secrets struggling for revelation to an unsuspecting world. And it seemed whatever was cooking was bound to boil over—one wondered only how soon.

But as the year grew to middle age some of the secrets could no longer be smothered, and the public pondered strange air disasters as it learned that planes and birds were not alone in the skies. Seven mysterious objects followed a BOAC airliner, saucers trailed the Secretary of Air, in Canada a thirteen-foot monster terrorized an Italian immigrant.

And out in space, now only 40,300,000 miles away, a great red eye was watching.

The Red Planet was in favorable opposition, closest to Earth since 1924, and what some saucer investigators had long suspected was now proven: with each approach of Mars during recent years, saucer sightings had grown in number. When Mars was far away in the summer of 1953, saucer sightings died down a bit, but in 1954 the sky was swarming with "unknown flying objects." The pattern of saucer sightings as related to Martian approaches was now definitely evident. Saucer enthusiasts wondered if the Mars Committee, which took off for Bloemfontein, South Africa, to study the planet telescopically from the better viewpoint available there, did not do so with an unnatural urgency.

I wondered why the Sunday supplements were not filled with news of Mars, now that surely there was a lot of good material available. Photographs would be clearer than before, undoubtedly, and feature writers once again could reflect on what Martians might look like.

But like saucer news, there also appeared to be a blackout on news about Mars. What the astronomers had discovered, they were not discussing.

And the impression could not be easily discarded that the Mars Committee was sitting on something big, something they did not feel it wise to release.

Dr. Warren Hickman, dean of Ohio Northern University, threw up his hands on saucers, announced that "Project A," set up within the University to reach some solution to the mystery, was no more.

Those in the know about Bridgeport gasped. Had the three men dared to silence a public institution?

If they had, Hickman was going along with the gag. He hastily issued a special bulletin stating that the University had not been ordered into silence. The Project had not been closed on request of the government, or, Hickman added cryptically, "some other organization." Saucer enthusiasts wondered just what "some other organization" might imply, since the dreadful possibility that some such power might exist was in effect being acknowledged by a noted academic leader.

Hickman's reason for ending the project somehow sounded familiar, as if a well-known source were writing his script. He said the project was being canceled because of the lack of reliable data from which conclusions might be drawn.

But in ringing down the curtain on saucers Hickman courageously, perhaps, made one pro-saucer concession.

"The information received by Project A," he stated, "indicated that a sizeable fraction of the total sightings throughout the country were sightings made of material objects. These material objects were not standard aircraft."

Here was a conclusion reached by a man skilled in objectively, open-mindedly assimilating and evaluating data. And he probably had IBM machines to help him reach this conclusion— but it was evident that as yet his machines were not rigged, adjusted in some Pentagonian manner to toss out the punched cards in a stacked deck, as some researchers hint the cards mentioned in *Project Blue Book Special Report No. 14* had been handled.

From a different part of the country another man raised his voice. In Washington, D.C., Mutual newscaster Frank Edwards made the needle on the decibel meter jump as he angrily asked his listeners why there obviously existed a censorship of saucer news.

Saucer sightings were frequently recorded in small, local papers but, strangely enough, such stories were not picked up and reprinted. One conclusion was inescapable: the news was being blocked in some way. Maybe it was voluntary censorship at work; maybe a direct order had been issued and was being obeyed. But somewhere a man with a blue pencil was drawing thick lines through the testimony of thousands of people. Occasionally the story of a sighting slipped through, but only when the man with the blue pencil had his tongue in his cheek, it seemed, for the stories that reached print in larger papers were obvious hoaxes, or accounts tricked up to sound ridiculous. Readers of these stories couldn't help discrediting them; the chances were that after reading of a hoaxed sighting, they would automatically brand all saucer accounts "suspicious."

After Edwards brought up the matter of saucer censorship, he saw the brass curtain lowering even upon him, slowly, perhaps, but nevertheless surely. At first the pressure had been subtle, but now it was growing severe.

He broadcast a frantic appeal to his listeners. Thousands of letters flooded the office of his sponsor, the American Federation of Labor, 500-to-one in favor of saucer news.

A week or two later Edwards got his walking papers.

Here might be a new angle on the three men, I thought. If they couldn't frighten someone into silence could they bring economic pressure to bear?

"D.C. is practically a police state," a prominent saucer book author was telling me over coffee in his Washington home. "I'm moving away from here quickly as I can. I could tell you more, but you wouldn't believe it. Call up Frank and ask *his* opinion."

The next time I talked with Edwards I asked him about it. I got an earful. He had produced a series of transcribed newscasts for sale to local stations, had secured a sponsor to back the project, but suddenly the sponsor had got cold feet.

It looked as if they had got Edwards too.

In midsummer I received a telephone call from Lucchesi. Since we had mutually acknowledged we had gone as far as we could on the Bender mystery unless new data showed up, we had been communicating less frequently.

"It's about time I heard from you, kid," I joked. "What's the matter you haven't written—the 'three men' got you or something?"

"No men in dark clothes, but several of the little green ones come here every week in funny little hats, carrying ray guns."

"You'd better be looking out for the men in the *white coats!*" I rejoined, but I could detect a serious note creeping into Dom's voice.

"Seriously, Gray, I just wanted to tip you off. I'm sending a fellow down to see you. He seems to be on the level, but yet —well, watch what you tell him, Gray."

Who was the fellow, I asked.

"He calls himself James Moseley, and says he's writing a book about saucers, though I get the idea the book deal is just a front, to give him an excuse to contact important people in research. The guy has no visible means of support, yet doesn't work at anything. Claims to be a millionaire, but if you'd see the car he's driving you wouldn't believe it. I believe he's in the pay of somebody—just wish I knew who."

I told Dom I got the pitch.

A day later Moseley walked into my office.

He was a pleasant enough chap. But a fellow who didn't want to talk about himself. For a saucer researcher that was a new twist.

He invited me out to dinner.

"Order anything you want," he offered.

I had steak.

228

"I'm new in saucer research," he confided, "and would like a rundown on just what you know."

I told him that was a long story, but I would answer specific questions he put if I were able.

Moseley was unusually curious. How long had I been publishing *The Saucerian?* What was my circulation? Did I have any absolute *proof* the saucers came from outer space?

He had postponed publishing his book, he said, but did plan to begin publishing a small saucer magazine similar to mine. To obtain some publicity he said he'd appreciate it very much if I would add his name to my staff on the masthead of *The Saucerian,* not that he would be able to offer me any real assistance, being busy, he expected, with his own publication.

"Titles are a dime a dozen," I told him. "I'll put you down as 'Eastern Editor' and occasionally reprint something from your magazine if it fits in."

He said that would be great.

For an individual of whose actual background I knew very little, I thought it unusual that I should immediately like Moseley. I still look him up occasionally when I am in the East, and he usually drops by Clarksburg on his somewhat enigmatic "trips to South America."

It is, therefore, perhaps likely that some of my close friends among saucer researchers are surprised when they learn that I really know very little about the man. For Moseley is now perhaps the most controversial figure enmeshed in the saucer mystery, and many people think that I should know what strange urgencies drive him to play down, obviously, it seems, interplanetary saucers in his publication, *Saucer News.*

Take Stringfield, for example, Leonard H. Stringfield, director of CRIFO (Civilian Research Interplanetary Flying Objects), who is recognized, I say almost enviously, as the most highly respected researcher in America today, and whose publication, *Orbit*, has shot to an amazing circulation figure.

I knew that something was running through the back of his mind all of that evening we spent together, and I wondered why he was hesitating to bring it up. Finally, after his charming wife, Dell, had put the two Stringfield children to bed, and everything was quiet in the house, Len cleared his throat.

"I've been meaning to ask you this all evening—don't answer if it violates a confidence. But what gives with Moseley?"

I knew he was getting at Moseley's strange statement in the November, 1954, issue of his publication.

"Honestly, Len, I wish I knew myself," I had to tell him.

I tried to explain that although most people thought Moseley and I were very close friends and that I should know everything about the promoter of the "Earth Theory," as he termed his odd and somewhat over-urgent debunking of interplanetary saucers, in actuality I knew very little about the man.

I didn't know, for example, just what Moseley's frequent trips to South America were for, though he had once told me a wild story about a search for a lost city.

I didn't tell Stringfield about my doubts as to whether Moseley had been to South America at all.

Like the time that I was half-pretending to pull Moseley's leg.

"Tell me, Jim," I asked with an artificial laugh, as if to make a joke of it, "why do you go to so much trouble having those occasional letters forwarded to me from Peru? Isn't it a lot of trouble to send the mail to some confederate there for remailing to me?"

Moseley turned white as a sheet. Then regaining his composure, he laughed and replied, "Yes, it is a lot of trouble. I just get a kick out of confusing you."

Stringfield had started me to thinking, however, and when I returned to Clarksburg I dug the complete set of Moseley's publications from my files.

Lucchesi and Roberts had helped Moseley launch the thing, though they dropped out later when the publication began to adopt a peculiar line. They had suggested its original title, *Nexus,* the title for a publication they themselves had once planned to issue, but had given up after the first issue when they found they did not have enough time to handle it. Moseley later changed the name of his publication to *Saucer News* when Augie and Dom thought it was time to disassociate themselves from the venture.

At the beginning Moseley's editorial line was pro-saucer, and he immediately gained a large readership, mainly, though, through advertisements in somewhat sensational "expose" magazines.

But something happened in late 1954 which completely changed Moseley's attitude about the mystery.

In his October issue Moseley came out with an article with a finalized title: "THE FLYING SAUCER MYSTERY—SOLVED."

"On a tip from Len Stringfield, of CRIFO, I have interviewed a nuclear scientist living in the New York area. This scientist, who has worked at the Los Alamos atomic energy plant, holds the highest possible government security clearances, and has made a detailed study of flying saucers."

That was how his opening paragraph began.

But Moseley's ending was the corker:

"The information I have discussed so far is a matter of public record. However, just before this issue went to press, I received irrefutable documented evidence which fully confirms these ideas. This information is due to a long-awaited leak from a high official source. It is now too late to assemble this startling data for this present issue, but it will be presented in full in the November issue."

I thought it was useless to telephone Moseley, but I did anyway.

"What is all this about, Jim?" I queried. "Can you give me what you have off the record? You know I'll respect your scoop, if you have one."

"Sorry, Gray, but you'll have to wait until you see the November issue."

I tried to cajole him into imparting some information, but he was adamant. Our conversation was complicated by some noises on the line.

"Don't mind that," Jim said to me. "That's only John. Hello, John, glad to know you're still with me."

Then he explained someone, he couldn't imagine who, had his line tapped. He had given whoever it was the name, "John."

"Oh, say, Gray, I just blew up a bridge yesterday! I have an atomic bomb I'm supposed to plant in the Pentagon next week."

There was a sharp click on the line. Whoever the tapper was, he had hung up.

"That's how I get rid of them," Moseley explained. "I start some wild tale of blowing up bridges and that always disgusts them."

"Really, Gray," he continued, "call it whatever you want, a 'shush-up' or my fear you'll scoop me, but I can't say anything more—you'll just have to wait for the November issue."

Moseley sent it air mail, special delivery.

I opened it rather breathlessly, I am afraid, but was disappointed and disturbed to find an editorial that sounded very much like Bender's last official announcement:

"In the October issue I stated, 'Just before this issue went to press, I received irrefutable documented evidence . . . due to a long-awaited leak from a high official source. . . .'

"I now owe my readers an apology. I must state that the documents referred to above are no longer in my possession, and that I am not at liberty to make any further references to them; nor am I permitted to elaborate as to why the information I promised you cannot be presented in this or any future issue. Suffice it to say that I simply am unable to publish this information, as much as I would like to."

Then another statement with a familiar ring:

"I would like to caution all flying saucer researchers to be extremely cautious in dealing with certain phases of the Saucer Mystery."

Bender, Jarrold, the others—now Moseley!

Somehow I felt the information Moseley promised would never reach the printed page.

And somehow I knew it would be useless to ask Moseley just what had occurred, just what he knew that he couldn't print.

The next time I saw him I didn't mention it, and he didn't either.

With that editorial a great change came over Moseley's publication. His editorial policy thereafter consisted of an attempt to thoroughly debunk saucers, interplanetary saucers, that is.

Thereafter *Saucer News* went to unnatural lengths to attempt to prove that saucers are made on Earth, are secret devices of various terrestrial governments.

When you read his material you could tell he himself didn't believe what he was saying. Hundreds of readers wrote to Moseley, picking his theories and articles to pieces; it was not difficult to do so.

I held a hurried telephone consultation with Lucchesi.

"Remember what I told you when I first sent him down there?" Dom asked me.

"Yes I do, you told me to watch him."

"That still holds true. If you have any new information about Bender, don't give it to him. It looks pretty obvious from here just who Moseley's working for."

"Who?" I asked, knowing what Dom would say.

"Who? The people you and I both know exist, but would give our right arms to have the real dope on."

The Silence Group.

What almost everyone in saucers knew existed, but couldn't put his finger on.

Someone who doesn't want the people to know about saucers. The government? We hoped so. We could go along with that.

Moseley evidently was visited shortly after he intimated he would publish his evidence. And obviously his visitors represented a powerful group, for Moseley was a man who impressed me as being someone who wouldn't scare easily.

"If they got Moseley, I think we should let it alone ourselves," Lucchesi confided. "Maybe we're into a field of investigation that's too hot for comfort!"

"That's not like you to say that." I told him. "Don't chicken out—remember that little slogan, 'To The Last Cup and Saucer?'"

"Don't worry, I'm still with you, but I hope that last cup isn't too hot to handle!"

We hung up.

Regardless of what Moseley knew and was not telling about, one thing was as visible as the nose on Durante's face. The three men were operating differently now—they must have realized how they had bungled the Bender case.

They weren't stopping investigators from publishing any more. That would be too obvious, and the public wouldn't stand for it, as they had found out from "working over" IFSB.

They had adopted a new policy.

They *encouraged* investigators to continue publishing.

Only they told them what to say.

Maybe they even subsidized them.

New York, Australia, New Zealand

Had someone "shushed up" Rockmore too?

His excellent publication, *Flying Saucer Review*, no longer was appearing, and he wasn't answering my correspondence.

That was odd, for Rockmore.

Elliott Rockmore had been nationally recognized as a sincere and reliable researcher. He had published an exhaustive list of saucer accounts arranged in chronological order. This provided other researchers with a reliable file on all important saucer sightings, and he was quoted widely in books and saucer publications.

Rockmore also had his feet firmly planted on the ground. He

was one of the first to expose "little men" hoaxes, and had helped me complete my files on a number of such cases that had occurred before I began building my own collection of data.

While in New York during December, 1954, I decided to dial Rockmore's Brooklyn number.

A woman answered the phone.

"May I speak to Elliott Rockmore?" I asked.

"Who is calling?"

I gave her my name.

"What *is* the nature of the call?" she inquired.

I explained that I was a friend of Rockmore's, that I published a saucer magazine.

The voice at the other end grew tense.

"I'm sorry, but he doesn't want to talk to anybody about the subject."

"But . . . I know Elliott very well, we're friends. . . ."

"I said I was sorry, that he does not wish to talk about it! Don't SAY it! WRITE it!"

The party hung up on me.

As Lucchesi said, it was a pattern all right. It looked as if all the key people were shutting up about saucers, one by one.

One question, though, bothered me.

I, myself, published a magazine of no little circulation. I had readers throughout the United States and in many foreign countries. For a private individual, I stretched myself pretty far.

Why hadn't the three men visited me?

I, too, had received the mysterious telephone calls, often with no one at the other end, that plague all saucer researchers, though I had usually credited them to cranks and harmless crackpots. At least I do not consider them important enough to set down here.

But no one had ever formally discouraged my work.

Why?

Maybe I just wasn't important enough.

But, more likely, I didn't have that certain piece of information. Or maybe that piece of metal from a UFO. Maybe it was because I announced, through the pages of *The Saucerian*, that I still had an open mind about saucers, and that I wasn't pushing any certain theory as final.

I often thought it might be worth being silenced and warned to keep quiet about what I knew if I could actually have something definitely *confirmed* as to the origin and purpose of the saucers.

Maybe I will some day experience that cold feeling of mingled satisfaction and fear, of triumph and defeat. I hope not.

* * * * *

It is perhaps superfluous to trace Jarrold's actions after an ominous and unpleasant visitor rang down the curtain on his unexpectedly revealing investigation of saucers. But for the record I think I should.

After I had gathered sufficient data on the IFSB closure I published a long and careful editorial in my January, 1954, issue, giving my readers a complete run-down on Bender's "shush-up."

Since I discussed Bender and Jarrold at some length, and reviewed charges from some quarters that they were perpetrating hoaxes, I hoped that the open-minded consideration I gave to this possibility would not anger the two men. It did not.

Jarrold wrote May 18, 1954, complimenting me on the fair way the discussion was handled. He also came up with another unusual statement.

"Although saucer publicity is now so anathemic to Al, I'm

sure that after a little reflection he will recognize this and will reply to your letters. Perhaps when next you write you might convey that point? If you like, you may at the same time ask Al whether there is anything in a story we have received to the effect that although he will not partake in any further saucer research, he *may* renew investigations into the objects now that they are known as UFO's. I hear that he is considering at least oblique—even if not *direct* interest in UFO's in the future again."

So Bender could discuss UFO's but not saucers? That was an interesting, if puzzling, statement.

But I couldn't see much difference in the two names, which had become synonymous terminology for the same thing.

I had noticed the Air Force preferred to label the phenomena as "UFO's" and didn't like the word "saucer" at all. Maybe that was because use of the latter terminology would be an admission that interplanetary space craft did exist.

Whatever Jarrold might have been driving at, Bender did not see it that way. Call them "UFO's," "saucers," "disks" or whatever you prefer, Bender still wasn't talking.

We must remember that regardless of what Jarrold had found out and confirmed to him, Bender evidently had not shared his secrets with the Australian investigator.

"I must confess that the closure of IFSB surprised me every bit as much as anyone else," Jarrold had written me.

Jarrold's communications became more infrequent and briefer, though his letter of May 31 may have been more significant than I recognized at the time of receipt.

"A couple of rumors have been causing us bother for the past week or so, holding that we have in our possession 'a piece of a flying saucer,' . . . 'a portion of a hostile missile.' "

Jarrold was referring to the unidentified objects observed over the town of Shepparton, Victoria, on the afternoon of May 12, 1954.

I don't know why Jarrold referred to the stories as "rumors," for he went on to relate how a portion of one of the several mysterious 30-foot objects had been forwarded to AFSB headquarters.

"It will be submitted for expert analysis in order to determine its exact composition and probable origin," though Jarrold added it might take several weeks to obtain a laboratory report.

"We had planned to release a full account of the Shepparton incident, but such rumors are at present deterring us, since we are still endeavoring to obtain further samples for analysis, and do not want the resident in question submitted to possible undesirable publicity in the meantime. Since the substance has not been examined by outsiders as yet, we do not wish to be officially associated with sensational claims before every scrap of actual evidence is in our possession to support.

"On the arrival of the results of the analysis projected we should be able to make a statement that cannot be elaborated upon or denied."

So Jarrold had his piece of metal!

Thereafter there was only dead silence about the analysis from ASFB, and soon there would also be the same silence from its president.

My last communication from Jarrold was dated July 15, 1954. It was somewhat hurried and formal.

"Recent developments of which I feel certain you will be glad to hear are that the Department of Air last month initiated a policy of referring specific sightings and theories to the AFSB for investigation, and where necessary, comment."

The famed Port Moresby pictures, a motion picture film of saucers in flight, were already in his possession, having been turned over by Air officials for his examination.

Jarrold had also received a communication from the Australian Minister of Air, suggesting he attend a meeting with Air Force Intelligence in Melbourne.

Since the communication was "highly confidential in nature" Jarrold was able to give me only a brief idea of its content. He was tied up in making travel arrangements, and would I please forgive the brevity of his letter.

The letter closed with the last paragraph of information to come from Jarrold before his exit from active saucer investigation.

"I must, before closing, convey that my trip should not be construed as involving any factor relating to public uneasiness regarding UFO intentions. It IS regarded here as being very satisfactory regarding general UFO research, and our own efforts in particular."

My next word about Jarrold came in a letter of April 20, 1955, written by Fred Stone, who had picked up the shattered bits of The Australian Flying Saucer Bureau and tried to put them back together with some degree of order.

Stone explained that for the past nine months Jarrold had made no reply to communications or response to "even the most urgent matters."

The rumor was going about Australia that Jarrold had been silenced by the government, but this seemed odd to Stone, who explained he had received very helpful and courteous treatment from officials. He had directed communications to Jarrold, asking him point blank if he was closed by security, but these letters, like all the rest, were not answered.

Stone had been president of the South Australian Branch of

the AFSB, and, in response to demands of the huge membership of the parent organization now without a leader, the former branch president effected a complete reorganization of the faltering association.

The new organization also had a new name, and this would help dispel the doubts, he thought, many people had developed about the former group. It would be called The Australian Flying Saucer Research Society.

In late 1955 I received a further communication from Stone which would represent Jarrold's final appearance in saucer research.

Stone's investigations into Jarrold's exit, he said, were now more complete, after a long trip to Sydney to interview some of the former's close associates.

He had established one thing as a definite fact:

Jarrold had not been closed down by the Australian government.

And Stone thought he had some of the real answers.

I will not go into the details of Stone's communication, one he feared I, being more of a materialist, perhaps, than he, would find too fantastic for belief.

But let me quote a part of his letter:

"Regarding the strange incidents quoted by Jarrold, I am fully convinced that they are most genuine—particularly the case of Harold H. Fulton (the mysterious odors and noises—G.B.).

"To assist you now I will say there are two distinct forces and powers at work. One trying to assist us and the other to destroy. One of darkness, one of light; positive and negative. Until you can get to the stage where clear discrimination between the two is possible any weird or strange thing can happen and much harm can come both to yourself and those around you. Jarrold is a clear case of one who refused to take this warning I sent him when he related his case to me."

So here we leave Jarrold, Bender, Moseley and the rest, their strange narratives yet incomplete. But perhaps with a little more light thrown on them.

For I do not like the talk of "forces" and "powers" and "darkness" and "weird or strange things."

I like to talk of things that I can understand. Things I can photograph and weigh and measure and maybe put into cages.

I like something that I can shoot at.

And so we come to the end of this book, one, perhaps, that you will not believe. I do not believe it either. It is something I do not want to believe, I tell you frankly, as I pound typewriter keys late at night trying to meet a publisher's deadline.

Perhaps there is no need for appending this one last letter, for you will not believe that I actually have it here in my files. You will not bother, perhaps, to ask to see it, and I do not blame you.

But here it is before me and I will include it. It is the swan song of John E. Stuart, formerly a saucer researcher who wrote on the letterhead of Flying Saucer Investigators. He does not use that letterhead now. The organization is broken up. Doreen Wilkinson has fled, her mind in confusion. Only John had the courage to write and tell me a part of it:

"Hi, there, friend. So long since I last wrote to you! And believe me a lot has happened too. So much, in fact, that Flying Saucer Investigators is no more! Yes, we have closed down.

"For a start, Gray, may I add my solemn advice to that of ———— ———— and Albert Bender? Then, for Pete's sake, take care of yourself and be very careful in your investigations!

"Mad? Well maybe I *am*. Sometimes I do wonder if it all did happen. However I know it did.

"I had a visit from a bloke who offered me some advice—after he had left I felt I should listen to what he said. You see I had a piece of grey-white metal and—well now I haven't got it! Our friend 'thought' he had more right to it than I. I have learned a lot about UFO's from this lad—oh yes he told me a lot—too much maybe, for my own personal safety.

"It is easy to understand, I think, why he told me what he did. It was meant to scare hell out of me—it did! I had plenty of fright in the last war and I am the first to admit that I was very scared after this 'gentleman' had left.

"No doubt, Gray, in due course I will tell them to go to hell, and take up saucers again. I don't know.

"You will be curious as to where I got my piece of 'metal.' It fell from a UFO. You have my report on the close sighting in June, 1954. In February of 1955 a similar sighting was made and from this I got my piece of metal. The next night, before leaving for Auckland, my visitor called on me.

"I can't, at the moment, tell you any more for it is too much for me to do. In short I'm not game to go against my 'orders.'

"All the best,

"And for God's sake be careful, Gray!"

In using the term, "the three men," people in saucer research have often spoken collectively of various visitors who have frightened flying saucer investigators into silence.

If these visitors have represented governmental authority we have temporarily condoned their actions, reserving judgment on their questionable methods. Perhaps the future will show these to have been justified.

If these strange visitors *do not* represent governmental authorities, then what fantastic sponsorship is responsible for their deeds?

As yet I do not have that answer.

I wish I did.

I may get that answer when information about this book begins to appear. I hope that the book is on the presses before that happens and that the presses will not stop. I think it is high time that this information, which I have up to now withheld from the public, were given to that very public for its consideration, its disbelief, its acceptance, or its action—however it chooses to react to the knowledge.

I have the feeling that I will accomplish more than just carrying out the duty of informing the public of what has happened. I have the feeling that from now on many people are going to creep out of the shells in which they have been hiding, thinking that they alone are burdened with a certain kind of fear. Not knowing that others, like themselves, have entertained unwanted and terrifying guests.

As long as you hide in your shell the three men, or one man, or whatever the case may be, will continue to deprive free men and women of their inalienable rights.

I doubt if our forefathers knew anything of flying saucers when they set up an immutable expression of our rights, but if they were living today, and heard stories such as I have told, I believe they would express their conviction that the freedoms they instituted or proclaimed could be interpreted to provide that their descendants have also the inalienable right to chase flying saucers to their hearts' content.

✱   ✱   ✱   ✱   ✱

There may be such things as flying saucers from space, and these things from space may have people or things in them that mean to do us harm.

We can fight these things off, somehow, with bullets, or prayers, or some new invention that we are bound to come up with if we have to. I am not alarmed about bug-eyed monsters, little green men, or dero who may or may not be shooting at us with rays from far underground.

Something else disturbs me far more.

There exist forces or agencies which would prevent us from finding out whether or not there are such green men, or bug-eyed monsters, or saucers with things in them.

I have a feeling that some day there will come a slow knocking at my own door.

They will be at your door, too, unless we all get wise and find out who the three men really are.

Appendix 1

The Shaver Mystery

"The Shaver Mystery" is the title given to a number of articles and stories, principally written by Richard S. Shaver, in which he theorizes that a degenerate race of people inhabit caverns beneath the Earth's surface.

"The Shaver Alphabet" appeared in the January, 1944, issue of *Amazing Stories*, a science fiction publication, and material by or about Shaver appeared in every consecutive monthly issue through the September, 1949, number.

Shaver said he disguised true stories as fiction in order to publish them. Two stories originally appearing in the magazine, "I Remember Lemuria," and "The Return of Sathanas," were later published in book form in 1948 by Venture Books, under the title of the first story. The book is out of print.

A new series of articles on "The Shaver Mystery" has been appearing in *Mystic* magazine, having begun in the October, 1955, issue. *Mystic* is published by Ray Palmer (who edited *Amazing Stories*) at Amherst, Wisconsin.

Appendix 2

Books About Flying Saucers

In presenting a list of other books about flying saucers, including, because of space limitation, only the most important works, neither author nor publisher necessarily endorses the claims, theories or contents included by the various authors. This list, alphabetically by author, is presented solely for the reader's reference.

*Adamski, George, and Desmond Leslie, *Flying Saucers Have Landed.* Adamski meets a man from Venus on a California desert. Leslie's section of the book contains theories based on historical references to saucers. Published 1953 by The British Book Centre, Inc.

*Adamski, George, *Inside the Space Ships.* Adamski's further contacts with space people, this time aboard their space ships. Published 1955 by Abelard-Schuman.

*Allingham, Cedric, *Flying Saucer From Mars.* Allingham claims to have witnessed a saucer land in Scotland and to have communicated with its occupant, a Martian. Published 1954 by The British Book Centre, Inc.

Arnold, Kenneth, and Ray Palmer, *The Coming of the*

Saucers. An account of Arnold's sighting of saucers over Mt. Rainier in 1947, and his investigation of a dramatic sighting at Maury Island, Tacoma, Washington. Published 1953 by Ray Palmer.

*Bethurum, Truman, *Aboard a Flying Saucer.* Bethurum visits the interior of a saucer at Mormon Mesa, Nevada, and talks to a beautiful woman captain, Auhra Rhanes. Published 1954 by DeVorss and Co.

Cramp, Leonard G., *Space, Gravity and the Flying Saucer.* Contains a theory of saucer propulsion by magnetic and antigravity forces, based on recorded sightings. Published 1954 by The British Book Centre, Inc.

*Fry, Daniel W., *The White Sands Incident.* Fry, a technician, is taken for a ride in a pilotless saucer. (Paperbound.) Published 1954 by The New Age Publishing Co.

Girvan, Waveney, *Flying Saucers and Common Sense.* The author minimizes the skeptic's case against saucers. Published 1956 by Citadel Press.

Heard, Gerald, *Is Another World Watching?* (Published in England as *The Riddle of the Flying Saucers.*) An early saucer book in which Heard advances a theory that saucers come from Mars and that Martians resemble insects, but with vastly developed intelligence. Published 1950 by Harper & Brothers.

Jessup, M. K., *The Case For the UFO.* Contains historical references to saucers and possibly allied phenomena, with a theory that saucers are permanent inhabitants of a point of gravitation neutral between the Earth and Moon. Published 1955 by Citadel Press.

Jessup, M. K., *The UFO Annual.* A collection of sightings for the complete year, 1955. Published 1956 by Citadel Press.

Keyhoe, Donald E., *The Flying Saucers Are Real*. First of a succession of saucer books by the retired Marine Corps major, and the first book to attract serious public attention to the phenomena. (Paperbound.) Published 1950 by Fawcett Publications, Inc.

Keyhoe, Donald E., *Flying Saucers From Outer Space*. Keyhoe's second book claims that information about saucers is being withheld from the public by the Air Force. Published 1953 by Henry Holt and Co.

Keyhoe, Donald E., *The Flying Saucer Conspiracy*. A continuation of ideas expressed in *Flying Saucers From Outer Space*. Keyhoe charges that a "silence group" exists within the Air Force, and that this group hides saucer information from the public. Published 1955 by Henry Holt and Co.

*Layne, Meade, *The Coming of the Guardians*. Contains a theory that saucers exist in another dimension of space-time and are piloted by entities termed "Etherians." Published 1954 by Borderland Sciences Research Associates.

Menzel, Donald H., *Flying Saucers*. Astrophysicist at Harvard College attempts to explain away all saucers as mistaken interpretation of natural phenomena. Many of Menzel's theories have been rejected by Air Force investigators. Published 1953 by Harvard University Press.

Ruppelt, Edward J., *The Report On Unidentified Flying Objects*. A report on governmental investigation of saucers during the author's tenure as head of the Air Force's "Project Blue Book." Published 1956 by Doubleday and Co.

Scully, Frank, *Behind the Flying Saucers*. One of the early saucer books. Bodies of little men from Venus are found inside a crashed saucer. Published 1950 by Henry Holt and Co.

*Van Tassel, George W., *I Rode a Flying Saucer*. The author claims to have contacted saucer pilots by telepathy or mediumship. (Paperbound.) Published 1953 by The New Age Publishing Co.

Wilkins, H. T., *Flying Saucers On the Attack* (Published in England as *Flying Saucers On the Moon*.) British researcher believes some saucers are hostile. Book contains records of many sightings. Published 1954 by Citadel Press.

Wilkins, H. T., *Flying Saucers Uncensored*. Continuation of content and theories published in *Flying Saucers On the Attack*. Published 1955 by Citadel Press.

*Williamson, George H., *The Saucers Speak*. Williamson and Alfred C. Bailey converse with saucer pilots via short wave radio. (Paperbound.) Published 1954 by The New Age Publishing Co.

---

* Denotes "contact" books, a term lately appearing in the rapidly-growing saucer terminology. The term designates those books in which meetings or communication with extraterrestrials is claimed and described. Such contact may not always be face-to-face; in some of the books so designated mental telepathy, radio communication, or mediumship is utilized.

Index

Adamski, George, 133
Aerial Phenomena Research Organization, 142
Air Force, 28, 39, 40, 69, 73, 74, 77, 80, 84, 85, 188-89, 223, 239, 241
Albuquerque, N.M., 40
Alexandria, Va., 147
Amazing Stories, 60, 64, 119
American Federation of Labor, 227
American Rocket Society, 146
Animals, reactions to saucers, 26, 161, 164
Antarctica, 166, 176, 213
Apro Bulletin, The, 142, 164
Arnold, Kenneth, 60, 148, 150
Atlantis, lost continent of, 62, 175
Australian Flying Saucer Bureau, The, 154-58, 162, 241-42
Australian Flying Saucer Magazine, The, 57, 157, 193, 196
Australian Flying Saucer Research Society, The, 242

Balocco, First Lieut. Edward, 39
Bat man, 41
Battrell, Mrs. Joyce, 47
Bender, Albert K.
  background, 68-70
  mysterious visitors, 92-93, 94-95, 112-14, 115, 123, 132, 135, 157, 158
  IFSB activities, 66-67, 87-90, 91, 97, 98, 99, 142
  advice to saucer researchers, 120, 138-39, 196
  theories, 117, 118, 121, 157, 166, 176, 189
  withdrawal from saucer research, 138, 239

  statements explaining silence, 126-27, 128-35, 151-53
  Saucerian cover, 137
  communications from, 109, 110, 144, 193, 194-95
  editorial statements, 68, 99, 138, 210-12
  references to, 58, 59, 60, 140, 141, 145, 146, 147, 154, 155, 162, 165, 177, 192, 197, 198, 203, 228, 233, 234, 235, 243
Bessemer, Ala., 41
Big Springs Weekly News, 79
Black, John Q., 36, 42-46, 49-51
Bloemfontein, South Africa, 225
Bowling, J. R., 48
Boyd, Lee, 183
Braxton Central, The, 18
Braxton Democrat, The, 28
Brewster, Jack, 107
Bridgeport, Conn., 66, 69, 87, 91, 96, 108, 136, 154, 202, 215
British Overseas Airways Corporation, 182, 224
Brown, Hugh A., 166-75
Brown, Lieut. Frank M., 148
Brush Creek, Calif., saucer, 37, 43-50
BSRA, 177-86, 188-90, 192
Byrne, J. Holt, 18
Byrd, Adm. Richard E., 166

Camera, Air Force, 40
Carlos, Mr. & Mrs. Joe, 48
Carr, Sheriff Robert, 19-20
Carson, Ethel G., 47
Chico, Calif., 47-48, 52
Civilian Saucer Investigation of New Zealand, 157, 161
Clips, Quotes and Comments, 190
Collier's, 30

Coming of the Saucers, The, 147-48
Conger, George, 82-83
Conway, S.C. sighting, 81
CRIFO, 229-31
Crissman, Fred L., 148-50
Curilovic, Mark T., 99-105

Dahl, Harold A., 148-50
Davidson, William L., 148
Daw, Rev. S. L., 90, 100, 117
Department of Investigation, IFSB,
    89-90, 95, 97, 99-101, 109
"Dero," 62-64, 146
Desvergers, J. D. "Sonny," 70-75
Deucalion and Pyrrha, 175
Douglaston, L. I., 166
Dove, Lonzo, 88, 100

Edwards, Frank, 75, 76, 226-27
Eisenhower, President Dwight D.,
    II, 144, 191
Etherians, 181, 188

Fate, 17, 19, 42, 66
Fawcett, George D., 118
FBI, 95, 97-98, 107-9, 127, 143-44
Fireballs, 90
Flatwoods, W. Va., "monster," 11-
    35, 42, 67, 70
Flying Saucer Investigators, 215,
    220, 243
Flying Saucer Review, 236
Flying Saucers (book), 56
Foley, Inspector, 107
Fort, Charles, 187
"4-D" Theory, 178, 182, 186, 221
Frame, Bailey, 31
Fulton, Harold H.,
    confidential files, 159
    information on Jarrold, 154, 158
    mysterious experiences, 160-61,
        242
    "Project X," 165, 212-14
    Bender questionnaire, 194

Gardner, Robert Coe, 52

Goodfellow Air Force Base, 80
Goose Bay, Labrador, 182
Government attitudes on saucers, 11,
    74-75, 148-49, 190-92, 223,
    226, 241, 245
Gray, John, 51

Hickman, Dr. Warren, 225-26
Hoard, G. D., 31-32
Holt, Rush D., 27
Hoover, C. E., 143
Hotel Statler, N. Y., 145
Howard, Captain James, 182
Hudson County (N. J.) Police, 102,
    106
Hyde, Mary, 147
Hyer, Tommy, 17

Irving, Nathan, 41

Jarrold, Edgar R.,
    mysterious visit, 153, 154, 155-
        57, 233
    joint project with IFSB, 157
    saucer theories, 158-59, 195-96,
        197
    mysterious experiences, 162-63
    "Project X," 165, 212-14
    letter from Bender, 193
    last saucer investigations, 238-42
Jersey City, N. J., 102, 111, 119
    141
Jordan, A. M., 18-19, 33
Jung, C. G., 123

Keenan, Thomas, 108
Kellegher, Lieut. 102-3, 106
King, Detective, 103, 107
Korea, sighting in, 39

Layne, Meade, 177-92
Lemon, Gene, 17, 22, 27
Lemuria, 62, 64, 175
Leyden, James, 82-83
Life, 64
Lingford, Charles, 180

"little men," 36, 42, 44, 45, 46, 57
Long Island, N. Y., 166
Lorenzen, Coral E., 142
Lucchesi, Armand, 103-5, 112
Lucchesi, Dominick,
    personality sketch, 81
    investigations for IFSB, 90
    and Curolovic Report, 95, 99, 100, 101-3, 105-8
    tape-letter to Barker, 110-22
    talks with Bender, 128-35, 137, 150, 154, 166
    and Shaver, 146-47
    and Moseley, 228, 234
    references to, 125, 126, 127
Luntz, Prof. Alfred, 180, 187

McDonnell Aircraft Corp., 184
Mantel, Capt. Thomas, 11
Mantong alphabet, 61
Mars, 133, 158, 181, 213
Mars Committee, 225
Mars, opposition of, 87-88, 210, 213, 225
"Mat" and "demat," 181-82, 184
Maury Island, 147-50
May, Mrs. Kathleen, 16-17, 22, 25, 29-30
May children, 17, 22
Mayell, Eric, 49
Menzel, Donald H., 11, 56
Meteorites, 18, 33
Mitchell Field, N. Y., 149
"Monsters," 12-35, 41, 67, 70-73
Moon, the, 137, 211
Morello, Ted, 149
Mt. Ararat, 175
Mt. Parnassus, 175
Moseley, James, 228-35, 243
Muroc Air Force Base, 190-92
Mysterious Investigators,
    interviews with Bender, 92-93, 94, 95, 114, 115, 119, 123, 129-30, 132-33, 135, 138, 152-53
    speculation on, 125, 126, 139, 140, 144, 147, 158-59, 205, 225, 226, 245-47
    interview with Dahl, 149-50
    interview with Jarrold, 153-57
    interviews with Smallwood, 201-9, 215
    fear of, 211
    technique used by, 235
    influence of, 233, 236-37, 241
    interview with Stuart, 243-44
    description of, 143, 208-9
Mystic, 66

Natalli, Ramon, 180
Neosho Daily Democrat, 77
New Haven, Conn., 90-91
New Zealand, 143, 154, 157, 158, 159, 215
Nexus, 231
Noah's flood, 174-75
Noises, strange, 161, 162, 164, 217-19
North Pole, 174
Nunley, Neil, 17, 21-27, 34

Oak Ridge, Tenn., 91
Odor, connected with saucers, 22, 25, 28, 70, 73, 162, 163
Ohio Northern University, 225
Olsson, Lieut. Robert M., 39, 40
Orbit, 230
Oroville, Calif., 48, 52, 55
Other Worlds, 66, 67

Palmer, Raymond E., 60-61, 64, 65, 66, 147-48
Palm Springs, Calif., 190-191
Partin, Deputy Sheriff Mott, 71, 73
Patton, Wilgus A., 38
Pentagon, the, 40, 75
"Phantom of Flatwoods," 34
Pittsburg, Kan., sighting, 76-78
Poltergeists, 41, 220
Popovic, George, 39
Port Moresby pictures, 241
Preston, Fred, 46
Probert, Mark, 179, 180, 188

"Project A," 225-26
Project Blue Book, 77, 226
Project Saucer, 12, 39, 148
"Project X," 165, 212-14

Radar sightings, 40, 184
Rear, Paul, 145-46
Rice, Mr. and Mrs. Allan, 47
Rockmore, Elliott, 236-37
Roberts, August C.,
  and Curolovic Report, 100, 102-3,
    105-8
  saucer photographs, 82-87
  investigations for IFSB, 90-91
  talks with Bender, 112-18, 120-
    21, 127-35, 137, 150, 154, 165,
    166
Robot, 34
Rogers, Mrs. Flora, 78-80
Russia, 211-12

Sanderson, Ivan, 18, 19, 32
Saucerian, The, 42, 52, 57, 73, 89,
  121, 137, 183, 204, 207, 224,
  229, 238
Saucer News, 229, 233
Saucers
  descriptions of, 45-46, 47, 70-73,
    76-77, 148, 183
  effect on religion, 90, 118, 123,
    143, 175-76
  interpretation of law, 51-52
  means of propulsion, 46
  noises connected with, 24, 44, 72,
    77
  photographs of, 83-86, 99-100,
    135
  related to psychology, 38, 52, 58,
    84, 123
  telepathic communication with,
    50, 194, 208
  theories of origin, 51, 57, 82, 88,
    92, 116, 117-18, 133, 134, 158,
    175, 180-82, 194, 212-13, 230
Science fiction fandom, 66
Shaver, Richard S., 60-65, 81, 111,

119, 130, 146-47, 208
Shaver, Ronnie, 17
Shepparton, Victoria, 240
Silence Group, The, 234
Sheehy, Barry, 57
Siberia, 171
South Pole, 117, 134, 166, 168-69,
  173, 176, 207
Smallwood, Gordon, 199-209, 215
Space Review, 68, 70, 75, 81, 88,
  98, 109, 115, 116, 117, 118,
  119, 120, 121, 138-39, 142,
  158, 165, 193, 210
Spade, Paul, 43, 44, 48-49, 52
Squyres, Bill, 75-77
Stewart, A. Lee, 17, 27
Stone, Fred, 241, 242
Stone, Mrs. Hannah, 47
Stringfield, Leonard H., 229-31
Stuart, John E., 215-22, 243-44
Sun, the, 141, 187
Sword of Damocles, 168
Sylphs, 147

Tacoma, Wash., 148, 149
Teleportation, 185
Temperature inversions, 40-41
"Tero," 64
"three men," *see* Mysterious Inves-
  tigators

United States Navy, 174
United States Rocket Society, 69

Van Allen, John J., 43-44, 46
Venus, 42, 181, 185

Walker, Mrs. Hilda, 40-41
Wilkinson, Doreen, 143, 215-21, 243
Willat, Thoreau, 49
Wright Patterson Air Force Base,
  39

Yada Di' Shi'Ite, 180, 187

Ziff, William B., 65